UFOs
THE GREAT
DEBATE

About the Author

A native of Minnesota but a resident of Colorado since 1969, Jeffrey Allan Danelek's life has been a journey that has taken him down many different paths. Besides writing, his hobbies include art, political and military history, religion and spirituality, numismatics (coin collecting), paleontology, astronomy (and science in general), and Fortean subjects such as Bigfoot, UFOs, and things that go bump in the night. His personal philosophy is that life is about learning and growing, both intellectually and spiritually, and that is the perspective from which he approaches each project he undertakes. Jeff currently resides in Lakewood, Colorado, with his wife, Carol, and their two sons.

To Write to the Author

If you wish to contact the author or would like more information about this book, please write to the author in care of Llewellyn Worldwide and we will forward your request. Both the author and publisher appreciate hearing from you and learning of your enjoyment of this book and how it has helped you. Llewellyn Worldwide cannot guarantee that every letter written to the author can be answered, but all will be forwarded. Please write to:

J. Allan Danelek
℅ Llewellyn Worldwide
2143 Wooddale Drive, Dept. 978-0-7387-1383-0
Woodbury, MN 55125-2989, U.S.A.

Please enclose a self-addressed stamped envelope for reply,
or $1.00 to cover costs. If outside the U.S.A.,
enclose an international postal reply coupon.

Many of Llewellyn's authors have websites with additional information and resources. For more information, please visit our website at www.llewellyn.com.

UFOs

THE GREAT
DEBATE

An Objective Look at Extraterrestrials,
Government Cover-Ups, and the
Prospect of First Contact

J. Allan Danelek

Llewellyn Publications
Woodbury, Minnesota

First Edition
First Printing, 2008

Book design by Steffani Sawyer
Book editing by Brett Fechheimer
Cover art © 2008 by Eva Serrabassa/iStockphoto
Cover design by Gavin Dayton Duffy
Llewellyn is a registered trademark of Llewellyn Worldwide, Ltd.

Library of Congress Cataloging-in-Publication Data
Danelek, J. Allan, 1958–
  UFOs, the great debate : an objective look at extraterrestrials,
government cover-ups, and the prospect of first contact / J. Allan
Danelek. — 1st ed.
    p.   cm.
  Includes bibliographical references.
  ISBN 978-0-7387-1383-0
  1. Unidentified flying objects. 2. Extraterrestrial beings. 3. Life on other planets.
I. Title.
  TL789.D24 2008
  001.942—dc22
                              2008035542

Llewellyn Publications
A Division of Llewellyn Worldwide, Ltd.
2143 Wooddale Drive, Dept. 978-0-7387-1383-0
Woodbury, Minnesota 55125-2989, U.S.A.
www.llewellyn.com

Printed in the United States of America

Other Books by J. Allan Danelek

The Case for Ghosts: An Objective Look at the Paranormal

Mystery of Reincarnation: The Evidence & Analysis of Rebirth

Atlantis: Lessons from the Lost Continent

contents

introduction

On the afternoon of June 24, 1947, Seattle businessman Kenneth Arnold was flying his private plane in the area of Mount Rainier, Washington, when shortly after 3 p.m. he saw what he described as a formation of brightly colored, crescent-shaped craft flying at speeds in excess of 1,200 knots. An experienced pilot and solid citizen, Mr. Arnold later described the vehicles to reporters as flying like a "saucer would if you skipped it across the water," thereby inadvertently coining the term *flying saucer*. Unbeknownst to Mr. Arnold, his curious sighting and casual description of what he encountered in the skies over Mount Rainier that afternoon sixty years ago started a worldwide fascination that not only launched the modern era of ufology, but has had profound and frequently divisive repercussions on the world of science that continue to echo to this day.

Not surprisingly, since then and right up to today, public reaction to the phenomena appears to be mixed. According to a recent

Roper poll,[1] about half the population believes extraterrestrials have or are currently visiting the planet, while millions claim to have experienced their own encounter with a "something" they can't easily explain. To some people, it has even become a type of New Age religion, with many imagining our alien cousins to be intent on helping us usher in a new era of peace and prosperity or, at the very least, helping to save us from our own shortsightedness—making the quest to understand the phenomena not just a scientific one but, in many cases, personal as well. For them, UFOs aren't simply interesting phenomena to be studied, but mankind's best hope for the future. It makes one wonder whether Mr. Arnold would have been so quick to describe his experience had he been aware of how his words would eventually morph into the billion-dollar industry it has become today and impact so many people on a deep, emotional, and, some may even hazard, spiritual level as well.

An equally substantial minority, however, consider the whole thing just so much nonsense: the stuff of fairy tales acceptable as light entertainment perhaps, but nothing to be taken seriously. Of course, it's not hard to understand such an attitude. How can we take anything like extraterrestrials seriously if we are constantly bombarded with every manner of crackpot and self-promoter—along with a host of New Age gurus and contactees of all ilks—intent on convincing us to not only believe their often fantastic stories but also hand over our wallets and common sense for the opportunity to do so? It's no easy task sifting fact from fiction and science from speculation, and as a result many simply give up and choose not to try.

However, despite all the patent nonsense that surrounds the controversy, I believe it is a subject that is too important to be casually dismissed, especially considering the substantial and growing body of evidence to support the possibility of extraterrestrial visitation as well as the implications of what it all would mean were it to

---

1. Roper poll prepared for the Sci Fi Channel, conducted in September 2002. See http://www.scifi.com/ufo/roper/ (accessed 6 August 2008).

be proven true. To do so would be, in my opinion, not only intellectually dishonest, but foolish. We *must* examine the issue, if only
for the sake of determining once and for all that there is nothing to
it. We owe future generations at least that much and, who knows,
perhaps at the end of the day, we'll have acquired a better understanding of our place in the universe in the process.

It has been my observation that far too many people who follow
the UFO phenomenon do so without carefully considering many of
the questions and the potential repercussions the issue entails—a
problem this book hopes to rectify. But this is designed to be more
than just another litany of UFO stories and page after page of grainy
photographs showing "something" flying through the air; this work
is designed to take a hard and, I hope, objective look at a phenomenon that has been such a major part of our culture for the past
sixty years. It is written for those who, like myself, are curious about
the possibility that our planet has been and may even now be the
subject of study to any number of extraterrestrial civilizations, but
who desire to get beyond the anecdotal stories, government conspiracy theories, and the general flotsam of faith such a phenomenon invariably produces. In contrast to most books on the subject,
the reader will notice that this work, while sympathetic to the idea
of extraterrestrials visiting our planet, holds the UFO community
accountable for what it's putting out to the public as fact. To that
end, in it I will ask the tough questions ufologists seldom consider,
such as is a space-faring civilization even scientifically credible and,
if so, why would it choose to traverse the vastness of space to study
us? And if it did, how likely is it that alien visitors could actually
operate in our skies largely unnoticed, much less possibly abduct
people from their cars and beds to conduct all manner of bizarre
procedures on them? In essence, then, this is not a book about what
happened, when, and to whom, but about *why* such things might
happen and what that could mean when they do.

This book also takes a careful look at the potential extent of
our government's role in suppressing information about this phenomenon and even considers the possibility that the military may

have salvaged saucers, and even alien bodies, in its possession. (It's always amazed me how millions of Americans can accept the idea that a saucer crashed near Roswell, New Mexico, in 1947, and that the government has been keeping the vehicle and its dead occupants on ice ever since, without once asking these most basic questions—an oversight this book hopes to rectify.) To this end, we'll briefly revisit the Roswell story, this most cherished legend of modern ufology, to see how it holds up in the face of scientific scrutiny, as well as explore some of the more technical concerns that recovering a crashed UFO would naturally incur. Most specifically, we'll look at the question of exactly how one goes about recovering a machine that could prove to be not only potentially toxic but also immensely destructive if mishandled. And, for that matter, we'll examine if it is even possible to "reverse engineer" an alien technology that might be centuries ahead of our own. And, finally, we will consider the question of why an extraterrestrial civilization would allow one of their disks and its dead crew to fall into our hands without making an attempt at recovering either—an extraordinary oversight, one would imagine, especially considering the repercussions such an inadvertent surrender of technology would mean to both sides.

In an effort to be as comprehensive as possible, this work will also attempt to make sense of all aspects of the phenomenon by examining some of the more modern mysteries frequently associated with UFOs, such as crop circles, cattle mutilations, and the mysterious MIBs (Men in Black). For instance, are the intricate patterns wrought in fields of corn and wheat around the world *all* the work of hoaxers, or are *some* of them messages from the stars? Are cattle mutilations merely misidentification of predatory marks on naturally deceased carcasses or is there something more sinister afoot? And what are we to make of the almost comical MIBs in their outdated Cadillacs, who seemingly appear from nowhere to question witnesses before disappearing again as suddenly as they appeared? Again, evidence of extraterrestrial visitation, a covert government agency at work, or simply constructs of vivid imaginations? And of course, no book on the subject would be complete without exploring the controversial issue of alien abductions, not simply in an effort to determine their validity, but in an attempt to better appreciate the way the entire phenomenon has reshaped the way we look at ETs.

Finally, a few words about myself may be in order, particularly with regard to what qualifies me to write on such a broad and expansive subject as UFOs, especially considering the fact that I am not a ufologist by trade or temperament. In fact, while I write on a broad range of paranormal subjects, my personal life has remained largely devoid of such experiences, making me, one would think, the last person on earth qualified to say anything on the subject. However, perhaps it's precisely this very *lack* of personal experience that makes me the ideal candidate to write on a subject like UFOs. As an outsider who has no axe to grind, no credentials on the line, and no agenda in mind, it allows me the luxury of looking at the subject from the unique perspective of a person who is neither a passionate believer nor a hardened skeptic. This makes it possible for me to walk the narrow path between both camps, note the strengths and weaknesses of each position, and finally attempt to fuse the two perspectives into a reasonable and, I hope, objective whole. I realize this is easier said than done, but it is my opinion that such is the only way by which we might begin to touch upon the truth that lies buried beneath the hype and sensationalism that so permeates the subject. Of course, I freely admit to having my own opinions where this subject is concerned, so everything on these pages must be taken with the understanding that I am not impervious to personal bias myself; however, I will strive to do justice to all sides and hopefully prevent my own prejudices from contaminating too much of this material. I leave it to readers to judge for themselves whether I have been successful.

I see extraterrestrials as a metaphor for the human condition, a phenomena that not only questions our role in a very large universe, but works as an outlet for our modern technologically driven worries and fears inherent to our rapidly developing planet. Whether we like to admit it or not, in many ways UFOs have helped define who we are as a species and have shaped our culture in ways we are just beginning to appreciate, and this book hopes to build a foundation upon which to explore the subject in a far more balanced and objective manner than is usually possible today. In the end, it is my hope the reader will find this a fresh approach to the subject that attempts to look at the issue from the position of reason rather than emotion. If I have accomplished even a small part of this goal, I will consider this work to have been a worthy endeavor.

PART ONE

The Case for Extraterrestrials

Is our planet really a vast playground for beings whose homes may be hundreds of light years from our own, as millions of people around the world contend, or are UFOs merely a product of our collective imaginations as many skeptics contend, and as such something we would be better off ignoring?

I suspect it would be as unwise to embrace either position with complete confidence. We simply can't afford either to casually dismiss the entire question of UFOs out of hand or blindly embrace them as real. Clearly there is something going on that demands serious study and, if possible, some sort of explanation. Sixty years of observations and millions of witnesses—many of them credible and levelheaded people not normally prone to hysteria, delusion, or exaggeration—simply can't be ignored, despite how extraordinary the claim that we are being visited—and possibly even abducted and contacted—by extraterrestrials may be. Considering the repercussions were it to be true (and the consequences were it to be demonstrated false as well) mandates that we take a closer look at the case both for and against the possibility that extraterrestrials may be in our midst and have been so for some time. To fail to do so invites complacency where the issue is concerned, which in the end could prove to be a greater threat to us than extraterrestrials could ever be.

To satisfy this goal, in the next few chapters we will not only briefly examine the history of UFOs but also consider the bigger question they pose from a cosmological and sociological standpoint. Most specifically, we will look at the question of whether intelligent life existing elsewhere in the universe is even scientifically feasible and, if it is, how and why such life might want to make the exhaustive journey to our world and take a look at us. We will also examine many of the objections and possible explanations frequently offered to explain away these sightings, not in an effort to debunk but in an effort to give all sides of the debate their voice. I believe that such is the only way to get to the bottom of this controversy and, in so doing, expand our knowledge about what has so often proved to be one of the most contentious topics of our time.

chapter one

The Debate Begins

L ate in the evening of March 30, 1990, radar stations in Belgium began picking up an unidentified, fast-moving target traveling over the town of Wavre, some twelve miles south of Brussels. Displaying no flight-data information and ignoring repeated hails, controllers eventually alerted a nearby NATO airbase, where the local commander decided to scramble a pair of F-16 interceptors to investigate the strange object. No sooner had the aircraft closed in on the target and begun attempting to lock onto it with their onboard radars, however, when the object suddenly accelerated to over 1,120 miles per hour—without creating a sonic boom—and began a series of high-speed evasive maneuvers the fighters were incapable of matching. For the next hour, the object—described by ground observers as generally triangular in shape—flew in a zigzag pattern over the city of Brussels just out of reach of the pursuing interceptors until finally, as if tiring of its high-tech game of tag (or perhaps having proven its point), it accelerated out of sight and disappeared into the night skies over Europe.

Subsequent investigation failed to ascertain precisely what the craft was, who owned it, or how it was capable of performing the maneuvers it did. Tapes from the F-16s' onboard radars showed that the object at one point descended from three thousand meters to twelve hundred meters in *two seconds*—a descent rate of 1,120 mi/hour, and at points accelerated from 175 mi/hour to 1,120 mi/hour in a few seconds—*an acceleration rate of 46 gs*.[2] Obviously, whatever it was, it possessed a level of technology far beyond our own, leaving the Wavre encounter one of the best-documented UFO reports in history and a mystery that continues to baffle experts to this day.

So what are we to make of such a story? It appears to have considerable "hard evidence" to support it: the object in question was tracked by several radar stations simultaneously, was recorded on the fighters' onboard radars, and was seen by literally hundreds of eyewitnesses, including military pilots, police, and other reliable witnesses. This makes it difficult to simply dismiss it as a hoax, a product of the imagination, or a misidentification of the planet Venus. Further, were it some sort of top secret research plane—either ours or the Russians—how could it perform such maneuvers or, for that matter, even make it deep into the heart of Europe, and be chased by NATO fighters no less, without *someone* knowing about it? Clearly, it appears "something" violated Belgian airspace, easily eluded the efforts of our most sophisticated fighters to catch it, and disappeared into the night sky as suddenly—and as swiftly—as it first appeared.

But what was it? Was it an extraterrestrial craft, possibly intent on testing the capabilities of our most advanced fighters, or could it have been something else? Obviously, we don't know—and probably never will. It's a classic mystery that defies efforts at either easy explanation or quick dismissal except, perhaps, by those so inclined to do so for reasons of convenience. However, while we don't

---

2. A *g*-rate far beyond anything the human body is capable of enduring, at least according to Professor Leon Brening—a nonlinear dynamic theorist at the Free University of Brussels—who extensively studied the data from the F-16 radar recorders.

know with any certainty what it was, we do know for a fact that the Wavre incident was not a unique, once-in-a-lifetime encounter. The decades have revealed hundreds óf similar stories, many recounted by veteran pilots, police officers, and even the occasional scientist, making it difficult to dismiss all of them out of hand, no matter how tempting—and convenient—that would be to do. It's clear that *something* is going on in the skies over our planet and, by some accounts, has been for a very long time.

But what are the chances that these craft may be extraterrestrial vehicles of some kind—craft of such technological sophistication and complexity as to make anything we might construct today look puny in comparison? Before any serious discussion of extraterrestrials can begin in earnest, a brief examination of the history of the phenomenon may be helpful if we are to have a proper foundation upon which to build our discussion. Obviously, recounting the history of UFOs in anything like a thorough manner would take several volumes, so for the sake of brevity this will be an extremely abbreviated look at just a few of the highlights that have shaped the modern "age of UFOs."

A Very Brief History Lesson

It has been my experience that most people consider UFOs a relatively modern phenomenon that seemed to arrive with the advent of the atomic bomb, but such is not the case. In reality, sightings of unidentified flying objects actually go back to antiquity and have been a part of the human experience since man first gazed into the heavens and noticed faint lights moving across the star-studded night sky. Reports of unusual aerial phenomena—"circles of fire" and "flaming chariots" in the parlance of the era—were being made by the ancient Egyptians as early as 1,500 BCE, while millennium-old Roman and Greek texts speaking of "fiery globes" and "circular shields in the sky" go back to the age of Homer. Even the Native Americans had their legends of "flying canoes" and "great silvery airships," with similar traditions having been a part of nearly every culture from the Far East to Europe. Renderings of objects that appear to resemble modern descriptions of disk-shaped UFOs can even be found on the walls of the famous Les Eyzies, Lascaux, and Altamira caves in France and Spain, which, in dating back to 15,000–30,000 BCE, suggest that this phenomenon has been around for as long as people have been on the planet.

Although this is a point that generates considerable debate among Christians, UFOs may even be mentioned in the Bible. While theologians are usually quick to dismiss such contentions, there are a number of observations in the Old Testament books of the Bible that might be interpreted as being extraterrestrial in nature. The book of Exodus, for example, records God as appearing as a "cloud" by day and a "pillar of fire" by night that moves before the ancient Israelites in their trek across the Sinai desert, a curious description that could easily be construed as a spacecraft as seen from the pre-technological perspective of the time. Additionally, the "flaming chariot" that spirited the prophet Elijah to Heaven (2 Kings 2:11) also appears to be a reasonable description of a flying saucer, if understood from an ancient perspective that lacked some context for describing things like aircraft or spaceships. But no biblical reference is as intriguing—or as controversial—as that described in the first chapter of the Old Testament book of Ezekiel:

> And I looked, and, behold, a whirlwind came out of the north, a great cloud, and a fire infolding itself, and a brightness was about it, and out of the midst thereof as the color of amber, out of the midst of the fire. Also out of the midst thereof came the likeness of four living creatures . . . their appearance was like burning coals of fire, and like the appearance of lamps: it went up and down among the living creatures; and the fire was bright, and out of the fire went forth lightning . . . Now as I beheld the living creatures, behold one wheel upon the earth by the living creatures, with his four faces. The appearance of the wheels and their work was like unto the color of a beryl: and they four had one likeness:

and their appearance and their work was as it were a wheel
in the middle of a wheel. . . As for their rings, they were
so high that they were dreadful; and their rings were full of
eyes round about them four. And when the living creatures
went, the wheels went by them: and when the living crea-
tures were lifted up from the earth, the wheels were lifted up
. . . When those went, these went; and when those stood,
these stood; and when those were lifted up from the earth, the
wheels were lifted up over against them: for the spirit of the
living creature was in the wheels . . . And when they went, I
heard the noise of their wings, like the noise of great waters,
as the voice of the Almighty, the voice of speech, as the noise
of an host: when they stood, they let down their wings.
(Ezekiel 1:4–24, King James Version)

While modern scholars generally interpret such writings as purely allegorical (or, more accurately, as a "vision" or type of divinely induced dream), it can't be denied that Ezekiel's description sounds very much like a flying saucer, especially to a man living in a technologically vacant and superstitious world. To an ancient man who possessed no concept of what a "spacecraft" was, using such terms as "wheels within wheels" and "God sitting upon a fiery throne" would make perfect sense. That doesn't prove that what Ezekiel saw was actually a UFO, of course (or that, by inference, God is an extraterrestrial), but it does suggest that the ancients, despite perhaps understanding such things in purely supernatural terms, may well have had encounters with things not of this world.

And the Bible is not the only ancient text that describes unusual aerial phenomena. The ancient Vedas of India,[3] for example, speak of flying objects known as Vimanas that sound very much like modern aircraft. Some of these accounts—many of them over three thousand years old (and probably transcribed from even earlier oral

---

3. The Vedas (Sanskrit for "knowledge") are a large corpus of texts originating in ancient India. They form the earliest layer of Sanskrit literature and are the oldest sacred texts within Hinduism.

traditions that predate them by centuries)—go so far as to describe the power sources these vessels possessed as well as the tremendous destructive power of which they were capable.

One of these epics, the *Rigveda*, describes one of these flying vehicles as a three-storied, triangular craft that could carry at least three passengers. Another book, the *Vaimanika Shastra*, even tells us how these machines were steered, what special precautions had to be taken on long flights, how the machines could be protected against violent storms and lightning, how to make a forced landing and even how to switch the drive to solar energy to make the fuel last longer! Further, the description of these machines are amazingly precise, with an unusual wealth of technical detail: the metals used along with their melting points, the propulsion units the various types of flying machines used, and a host of other surprisingly complex details. For example, one account tells that the Vimanas were constructed from three different types of metals, which they called *somala*, *soundaalika*, and *mourthwika*, and which, if mixed in the right proportions, produced sixteen kinds of heat-absorbing metals with names like *ushnambhara*, *ushnapaa*, and *raajaamlatrit* (words that, unfortunately, cannot be translated into English). Seven types of engines are also described, with the special functions for which each are suited and the altitudes at which they work best, giving the modern archeologist's insistence that these "aircraft" were simple allegories or fanciful descriptions of "air gods" difficult to accept.

While I suppose it's possible that the ancient Indians possessed a remarkable—and unusually technologically sophisticated—imagination the likes of which would not be seen again until the writings of H. G. Wells appeared in the nineteenth century, it is difficult to dismiss at least the possibility that these people were describing what can only be considered highly complex aerial machines thousands of years before the earliest industrialized civilizations had taken root. Whether they were terrestrial (shades of an Atlantean civilization?) or extraterrestrial in nature is another question;

in either case they appeared to be seeing something well beyond the breadth of what they should have at the time, making the true nature of the Vimanas one of the enduring mysteries of the age.

From Airships to Foo Fighters

But it wasn't until the dawn of the twentieth century that unidentified aerial vessels of some kind or another first began edging their way into both our skies and our collective consciousness. Perhaps the earliest well-documented incident of a "something" appearing in a sky that should have been devoid of any man-made objects occurred late in the autumn of 1896, when residents of California began reporting "airships" in the skies over Sacramento and San Francisco. Usually described as cylindrical or cigar-shaped by most witnesses, the often brightly lit vehicles were usually slow-moving, though on occasion they could be seen to speed up dramatically and vanish in seconds. Other witnesses reportedly saw these craft land and even told of carrying on lengthy conversations with their very human occupants, who seemed quite willing to describe their vessel's inner working in some detail and even, on occasion, give guided tours. Later, these mysterious vessels began appearing in the skies over the Midwest, where they continued to generate considerable controversy throughout the spring of 1897 before abruptly disappearing in April of that year.

Of course, many explanations have been offered for what these "vessels" may have been—a splitting comet, the planet Venus, lit balloons, even evidence of early airship development by parties unknown—but none of these seemed sufficient to explain away the most credible of the accounts. Journalistic hoaxing—perhaps encouraged by earlier reports of the mysterious craft—and even cases of mass hysteria undoubtedly accounted for a large number of sightings, making it easy to dismiss the entire incident as the product of the era's "yellow press" and the country's penchant for tall tales, but that too seems an overly simplified explanation. Clearly, it seems that *something* would have needed to have appeared in the skies over America for several months in the final years of the nineteenth century to get the whole thing started, yet no adequate explanation has ever been found, making the "airships" of 1897 as much a mystery today as they were in our great-grandparents' time.

It wasn't until World War II, however, that modern-type UFOs were first reported, when Allied air crews first began encountering something they nicknamed "foo fighters" trailing and sometimes even charging their formations. These fast-moving orbs of light, usually no more than a few inches in diameter, were often seen to make erratic, impossibly sharp turns and zoom along at speeds of nearly five hundred miles per hour, giving them the effect of being not only powered craft of some kind but also devices that appeared to be under intelligent control.

At the time, Allied bomber crews, who often saw them in considerable numbers during daylight bombing raids over Germany, thought they were Nazi secret weapons (sometimes even referring to them as "krautballs"), and the fact that they largely vanished shortly before Germany's surrender—suggesting the plants that made them had been overrun by advancing Allied armies—would seem to support that contention. However, an exhaustive search of German records after the war failed to find any record of such a weapon in the Nazi arsenal. Further, it doesn't explain how, even if they were of German manufacture, such small devices—most no larger than basketballs—could achieve such high speeds or be remotely piloted with the primitive technology available at the time. Additionally, if the Nazis did possess such a remarkable technology, why didn't they use it to create something more useful than apparently harmless little orbs of energy? Such a capability should have made it possible for the Germans to have produced an extremely potent weapon—something akin to an early air-to-air missile, perhaps— with which to bring Allied bombers down, but the little foo fighters did little more than occasionally unnerve air crews with their aerial antics, making their value as a military weapon questionable. The fact that they were also seen over the Pacific also argues against them being of German manufacture, plus the fact that they were reported by Axis air crew as well—who similarly thought they were Allied weapons of some type—further deepens the mystery.

Modern explanations chalk these little orbs of energy up to ball lightning—a somewhat unusual but not entirely rare phenomena in which balls of ionized gases sometimes form spheroid-shaped balls that glow brightly, appear to be attracted to the electromagnetic signature of metal aircraft (giving them the appearance of being under intelligent control), and are known to zoom away at high speed or even explode. Certainly, this appears to be a reasonable explanation, though it does seem strange that the phenomena didn't appear until fairly late in the war and that they somehow managed to disappear right around the time it ended. One would imagine they should have been seen fairly regularly both before and after these periods as well, making the ball-lightning hypothesis not entirely satisfactory.

Start of the Modern Era—The Arnold Sighting

Though newspapers reported on sightings of "ghost rockets" over Scandinavia in the summer of 1946,[4] the modern era of ufology actually began with Kenneth Arnold's sighting of a formation of strange craft over Mount Rainier, Washington, in June of 1947. Flying on a business trip from Chehalis to Yakima, Washington, in a small private plane, Mr. Arnold saw a series of bright flashes in the distance off to his left, flying in a long chain. For a moment, he thought they might be a flock of geese but quickly ruled this out due to their altitude, bright glint, and obviously very fast speed. He then thought they might be a new type of jet and started looking intently for a tail and other flight surfaces, but was surprised when he couldn't find any. In any case, the formation quickly passed in front of Mount Rainier, where they appeared dark in profile against the bright white snowfield covering the mountain, though they still

---

4. These were thought at the time to have been Soviet missile tests, but their true nature and purpose was subsequently never explained.

occasionally gave off bright flashes of light as they flipped around erratically.

Generally, he described them as crescent-shaped and estimated their angular size as about sixty feet—an estimate that was later upgraded by Air Force analysts to 140 to 280 feet based upon analysis of human visual acuity and other sighting details. Although moving on a more-or-less level horizontal plane, Arnold said the objects weaved from side to side "like the tail of a Chinese kite," darting through the valleys and around the smaller mountain peaks, where they would occasionally flip or bank on their edges in unison as they turned or maneuvered, causing almost blindingly bright or mirror-like flashes of light. Curious about their speed, he began to time their rate of passage: noting that they moved from Mount Rainier to Mount Adams—a distance of about fifty miles—in one minute and forty-two seconds (according to the clock on his instrument panel), he later calculated their speed to be just over 1,700 miles per hour—about three times faster than any manned aircraft had flown by 1947.[5] The encounter gave him an "eerie feeling," he later recounted, but at the time Arnold suspected he had seen test flights of a new U.S. military aircraft, a prospect that seems unlikely considering the fairly primitive state of military aviation at the time.

In any case, whatever it was that Mr. Arnold encountered over Washington state that June afternoon turned out to be more than just a strange anomaly worthy of only a brief mention in the local press. It was the astonishing speed, in addition to the unusual saucer or disk description, that seemed to capture people's imagination and sparked what was to become a worldwide "craze" that was to result in thousands of people from all walks of life coming forward over the next few months to recount their own stories of having seen inexplicable objects in the skies very much like Mr. Arnold's

---

5. Not knowing the exact distance where the objects faded from view, Arnold conservatively and arbitrarily rounded this down to 1,200 miles an hour, which was still faster than any known aircraft of the time.

"disks." Though largely lampooned by the media and the scientific community, almost overnight "flying saucers"—as the press immediately labeled them—turned into a global fascination, and suddenly a subject that would have been dismissed as nonsense a mere decade earlier became a phenomenon that shows no signs of letting up anytime soon.

Of course, Kenneth Arnold can't take all the credit for kicking off the modern age of ufology; considering the Cold War paranoia of the times, it was inevitable at some point that these mysterious objects would have come into the public consciousness. What made this encounter over sixty years ago different was the public's reaction to it and how it went on to shape our culture in both subtle and significant ways—especially in Hollywood, which was to use this new fascination with "men from outer space" to fill movie screens throughout the 1950s with a litany of movies of usually dubious quality. In spite of this, however (and, perhaps, in part *because* of it), most people still dismissed UFOs as so much nonsense, though no one could deny the fact that regardless of what one thought of the issue, UFOs were here to stay—at least in the imagination of the general public.

From Contactees to Conspiracies— An Overview of Sixty Years of UFOs

Obviously, producing anything like an exhaustive timeline of the phenomenon from 1947 through today would be a massive undertaking, so I will not attempt it. However, to get a better overview of how UFOs have evolved from a mere curiosity into a full-fledged phenomenon, I believe it is possible to divide the last sixty years into roughly three specific phases or "eras" that seem to have well-defined aspects unique to each of them. These phases don't possess unambiguous start-and-end dates, of course, and some of them overlap or are ongoing today, but they should serve as a means of helping us understand the evolutionary steps ufology has taken since its inception in 1947.

The first of these phases or periods could be called the *contactee* era, which began somewhere near the end of the Korean War and ran strong throughout the 1950s and early 1960s. This was a period marked not only by a rapidly growing interest in the phenomenon by the general public, but it was also a time when a small but enthusiastic handful of men and women made names for themselves by claiming to having been contacted by extraterrestrials—claims that included not only being in direct communication with the occupants of UFOs but even of being taken for tours of the solar system in their fantastic craft. Perhaps the most famous of these contactees was a hamburger-stand owner, George Adamski, who claimed to have encountered, in the California desert in the fall of 1952, a conspicuously human-looking Venusian man by the name of Orthon. Warning him of the dangers of nuclear war, Orthon then graciously took Mr. Adamski on a tour in his spacecraft of the immediate planets (including his own Venus). Producing a number of photographs of the alien ships (subsequently demonstrated to having been a canister lid off an old vacuum cleaner) and authoring several books on the subject of alien visitation, Mr. Adamski not only made quite a name for himself but also dutifully continued to carry out his duties as a sort of "interplanetary ambassador" with zest and determination right up to his death in 1965. Though a few other contactees also made names for themselves as well, none has proven as capable of capturing the public imagination the way the colorful and prolific Mr. Adamski was able to do, making the man one of the true pioneers of the phenomenon.

Of course, most people dismissed the contactees' claims as products of overactive imaginations, delusional personalities, or publicity-seeking, but these claims did manage to reshape the way we looked at the prospect of aliens in general. Despite what many imagined, they were not evil invaders intent on conquering and enslaving the human race but rather beings of great compassion and concern for our planet. As such, it's difficult to understand how the period became so synonymous with fear of extraterrestrials. Whereas in the 1940s we saw them as mere curiosities, within a decade they had become mysterious visitors of uncertain and possibly hostile intent, despite the assurances of many of the contactees that they were anything but malevolent. Apparently, even a positive message was not powerful enough to overcome the Cold War–based fears of the time, leaving the 1950s and early 1960s an era that perceived ETs to be essentially warlike and even sinister in nature.

In such a climate, then, it's not difficult to see how extraterrestrials morphed from merely potential threats into very real ones, launching what I like to call the second—or *abductee*—age of the UFO era. This period, which started sometime in the mid-1960s and in many respects continues today, began with the remarkable story of a New England couple by the name of Barney and Betty Hill who, in September 1961, claimed to have been not simply contacted by aliens, but forcibly abducted by them while driving through the White Mountains of New Hampshire. Although neither remembered an abduction experience at the time (in contrast to contactees who usually claim complete recall of their experiences), the Hills began having increasingly frightening dreams of having been taken into a spacecraft by decidedly nonhuman-looking creatures and being subjected to various bizarre and painful procedures. Eventually these extraordinarily vivid dreams became so disturbing that the couple was compelled to seek psychiatric help in an effort to learn the reason for the unusual shared trauma. It was only later, under hypnosis, that their stories—curiously paralleling each other although they were questioned separately—emerged, serving as a springboard for what was to become an entirely new, and even more sinister, aspect of extraterrestrials.

Though the Hills' account was ultimately debunked by skeptics (it is thought the couple may have been influenced by an *Outer Limits* episode that featured a very similar abduction scenario—

and aliens—as the one the Hills described under hypnosis[6]), the "abductees," like the "contactees," were also soon to have a major impact on the way we perceived extraterrestrials. Whereas up to then we usually pictured them as very human in appearance (à la Klaatu from the 1951 classic *The Day the Earth Stood Still*), the Hills described aliens who were decidedly nonhuman in appearance and behavior, even to the point of having oversized eyes that wrapped around the sides of their heads. Additionally, while contactees were chosen by their hosts to tell the world about them and their warnings of impending worldwide catastrophe, abductees routinely had their memories wiped (or, more correctly, suppressed), apparently in an effort to hide their nefarious deeds. In effect, then, abductions became the "darker" side of the phenomenon, and remain so to this day.

The Hills' story had other effects as well, the most important being to serve as a type of "blueprint" for later accounts, eventually resulting in many hundreds or—by some estimates—thousands of people coming forward to make similar claims over the succeeding decades. Perhaps fueled by such books as author Whitley Strieber's bestseller *Communion* in 1987 (in which he describes a series of incidents in which he was spirited away by tiny little creatures to a medical facility of some type), many of these accounts include not only reports of people having been abducted and examined by aliens, but even of women abductees being artificially impregnated and giving birth to hybrid alien/human fetuses. While such stories appear to have waned by the end of the 1990s, they are still occasionally recounted today, usually by people under hypnosis and often many years or even decades after the traumatic event. Whether such claims can stand up under careful inspection will be discussed later, but for now it is enough to recognize that with the start of the abductee era, aliens went from being our friends and

---

6. It was never entirely clear, however, how the Hills managed to share their dreams. Conventional wisdom suggests that one likely influenced the other by recounting his or her nightmares, thereby inadvertently influencing the other to have similar dreams, complete with the identical imagery described.

benefactors to something to be feared and even dreaded, casting a more malevolent pall over the entire phenomenon.

But things were to get even darker within the UFO community. Considering the political instability of the 1960s and 1970s, it was inevitable that the UFO phenomenon would eventually move down a path in which the government would become the villain to many people, resulting in the third and current phase of ufology, which I like to call the *government conspiracy* phase.

Of course, suspicions that the government and military were covering up what they "really know" about UFOs has been a part of UFO lore from the beginning, but it wasn't until shortly after the termination of Project Blue Book in 1969 (we will examine the extent of official government involvement in the phenomenon in chapter 7) that such fears became more pronounced. These suspicions were soon fanned to white-hot in the 1980s with the introduction of the Roswell incident (an alleged saucer crash and recovery made in New Mexico in 1947), and still today the idea that the government not only knows considerably more about UFOs than it is telling but is also actively engaged in a concerted effort to keep that information from the public is a common belief among many in the UFO community.

What makes this current phase so unusual is not merely its inherent distrust of government in general but also some of the more extraordinary claims some ufologists have made over the last thirty years, largely as a result of this presumption. Probably the most astonishing allegation is that the military has recovered a number of crashed disks and has been studying them at secret labs around the country in an effort to integrate their technology into our own—an allegation that started with the supposed recovery of a single craft at Roswell and has since grown in scale until today some ufologists maintain that literally scores of UFOs have crashed and been recovered over the course of the last sixty years. Even more extraordinary is the related charge that, in addition to crashed alien hardware, the military also has recovered the bodies of dead aliens as well, which it is also keeping carefully hidden from public view. Of course, the military consistently denies both assertions, but despite that—and, quite possibly, *because of it*—the idea that the government has dozens of recovered disks—along with an indeterminate number of their dead occupants—has become a major tenet of faith among hardcore ufologists.

It's no wonder, then, that some claim we are in the midst of the "crazy era" of UFOs—a charge not entirely unjustified in a world that sometimes appears to have lost its logical yardstick. As such, even though ufology has clearly come a long way since the early days of contactees describing their visits to Venus and grainy and often highly suspect photos being touted as "proof" of extraterrestrial visitors, it still has far to go—and many obstacles to overcome—before science is likely to start paying attention.

Conclusions

While admittedly this is only a quick sketch of the last sixty years of ufology, it should be sufficient to at least serve as a good starting point from which to launch our study. If nothing else, it should make it apparent to even the most casual observer that UFO sightings have become so common over the intervening decades that they no longer surprise us when they make their way into the paper or onto a newscast. It seems that, for whatever reason, the prospect of visitors from the stars continues to intrigue a large segment of the public, who has grown so comfortable with the idea that alien visitors might be orbiting our planet that many have long since learned to regard them in a curious sort of way as a natural part of our environment.

What's important to recognize in all of this, however, is that despite the best efforts of the skeptical and science communities to debunk the whole affair, it seems apparent that there is more to the phenomenon than science is willing to admit. In spite of all the silliness the issue has dredged up over the years and irrespective of the escapades and patent nonsense exhibited by many of its most rabid proponents, if anything the phenomenon appears to be growing more robust all the time, taking on a size and scope that has since rendered it incapable of being ignored. For better or for worse—and whatever they are—UFOs may in turn fascinate, amuse, annoy, or even frighten us, but whether we want to admit it or not, UFOs are here to stay.

chapter two

Is There Life Out There?

Sometimes I think the surest sign that intelligent life
exists elsewhere in the universe is that none of it has
tried to contact us.
    —Bill Watterson, creator of *Calvin and Hobbes*

Before any discussion of extraterrestrial life can begin in earnest, it is first necessary that we ask the most basic question that can be asked, and that is whether there is a reasonable chance that intelligent life *could* exist elsewhere in our galaxy. Clearly, unless we can establish that there is at least the possibility that advanced life exists and that, further, it possesses a space-faring capability that makes it possible for such beings to visit us, any further discussion of extraterrestrial visitation remains pointless. As the pivot point around which our entire study revolves, then, such a query is the most logical place to start.

For most of history, humanity generally rejected the notion of intelligent life—except for angels and demons—existing apart from our own planet. We were God's special creation, it was believed, a unique, one-time experiment around which the rest of the universe appeared to revolve. Even the very thought that there were other planets besides those handful we could trace across the night sky— much less sentient creatures like ourselves possibly living upon them—seemed not only most unlikely, but to religious authorities, even blasphemous. As far as both science and religion were concerned, we were it.

That perception changed, however, both as the mechanism that generates life became less supernatural and more biological and as astronomers began to expand the borders of the perceivable universe (as well as when a growing willingness within religion to expand the boundaries of "God's creation" began emerging). Of course, at first the question of whether other planets existed outside our solar system—while largely assumed—had to be demonstrated, which it finally was in 1995, when a Swiss team of astronomers discovered the first true extrasolar planet orbiting the star 51 Pegasi some fifty light years away. That single discovery was the fuel that gave those who believe life to be ubiquitous reason for hope, for now it meant that our solar system—with its eight planets and dozens of moons—was not unique in the universe. Since then, nearly two hundred extrasolar planets have been found, a number that as our means for locating such planets improves will only increase exponentially, further enhancing the idea that the process by which solar systems form appears to be universally consistent. Naturally, this implies that the Milky Way galaxy, itself just one in an ocean of galaxies, could be home to many hundreds of billions or even *trillions* of planets and moons of all sizes and descriptions—making the prospect for life existing outside our own solar system not only very good but practically assured. Of course, the vast majority of planets will be inhospitable to life of any kind, but if even a tiny percentage of them are temperate enough to sustain at least the possibility for life, we're still talking many millions of planets, providing us a stage upon which to consider that advanced alien races may conceivably exist.

But estimating the total number of planets in the galaxy and determining how likely there is to be life on any of them—much less intelligent life—are two different things. There are those who maintain that life—even on a microbial scale—is so complex and subject to so many variables that the chances of it evolving elsewhere are infinitesimally small. Though this position is more generally maintained by creationists in an effort to bolster their claims that life is a one-time divinely inspired act of creation, there are those inside the scientific community who hold to this position as well, mandating that we would be wise to examine this claim carefully before continuing our quest.

All Alone or a Crowded Universe?

It is undeniable that life on Earth is a byproduct of a complex and unique chain of circumstances working together, without which life—at least on a complex multicellular level—would have been impossible. The distance of the earth from the sun, the position of our system within the spiral arms of the Milky Way, the amount of sunlight and cosmic radiation our planet receives, water content and availability, and even things like plate tectonics, the size and distance to our moon, and our own sun's distance from our nearest stellar neighbor, all had to be precise in order for us to be here. Make the ozone layer just a little thinner, move us a couple of million miles closer to the sun or make our orbit even slightly elliptical, and life as we know it would never have emerged—much less evolved. We truly are a byproduct of many elements coming together at precisely the right moment, without which Earth remains a lifeless chunk of rock orbiting a rather unspectacular star on the outer fringes of a very large galaxy. As such, the likelihood that such ideal circumstances could be duplicated elsewhere in the cosmos seems not only remote but practically impossible, thereby dramatically reducing the chances of highly developed life emerging elsewhere in our galaxy (or, perhaps, even throughout the universe).

In essence, we are a once-in-a-trillion long shot unlikely to be replicated again.

That, in a nutshell, is what's known as the Rare Earth argument, and despite being championed by a small number of prominent scientists, it remains the minority view within the scientific community. Most find it too restrictive and unimaginative, and point out that since simple organisms have been found to flourish in environments previously thought inhospitable to life here on Earth (such as beneath twenty-foot-thick sheets of Arctic ice or around superheated hydrothermal vents on the ocean floor), life may be hardier and far more resilient than first imagined. With that in mind, then, some suggest that life should be possible almost anywhere in the universe provided that certain basic parameters of temperature, gravity, atmosphere, levels of cosmic radiation, and the presence of liquid water—among other factors—are all met. This, also in greatly simplified terms, is what's known as the Common Earth argument, and is the hypothesis that appears to be proving increasingly popular within the scientific community.

Both theories suffer from one major problem, however, and that is that they're limited to the observations of a single planet (our own), making how we interpret the emergence of life here the main determiner for which position we embrace. The Rare Earth theory is quite correct in its observation that many factors had to be precisely aligned in order for life to emerge on this planet, but it fails to take into account that there is nothing that definitively precludes the possibility of complex life emerging in other environments. Even the necessity that life be carbon-based is not absolute: many have speculated about the possibility of silicone- or ammonia-based organisms, making the prospects for life even better.

To assume life to be capable of existing under even the most severe and inhospitable environments, however, has its own difficulties, chief among them the inability to explain the process by which carbon-based life could emerge under less-than-ideal conditions or how silicone- or ammonia-based life forms might be possible. Without more than the single model—Earth—to study, and recognizing our still very limited knowledge of what may be out there, we simply can't say with any degree of certainty what is and is not possible as far as the emergence of life is concerned.

As such, scientists have fallen back on statistical probability to pin their hopes to. Different approaches are used, but it works basically from the premise that even if only a tiny fraction of all planets in our galaxy are potentially capable of harboring life on any level, and if even a tiny fraction of these—say 1 percent—have such life, the number of potentially life-bearing planets in our galaxy alone— a galaxy of between two hundred and four hundred billion stars and potentially a trillion or more planets and moons—would be in the *billions*. As such, even if life is a one-in-a-million long shot, given billions of chances for it to occur, the odds are good that life is not only possible but, possibly, abundant.

However, while science has generally come down on the side that life is statistically probable elsewhere in the universe, few, it seems, are willing to go on record as accepting the possibility that any of it may be advanced, much less intelligent. Yet this reluctance strikes me as being more of an article of faith than science; if life is possible on *any* level, there is no logical reason it couldn't evolve into increasingly more complex organisms up to and including, ultimately, sentient beings. We know that intelligent life is possible based upon what happened here on Earth; logic, therefore, dictates that if it can happen once, it should be capable of happening again, thereby rendering the assumption that mankind is a unique accident incapable of being replicated elsewhere under similar (if not identical) conditions a weak one. It's a bit like maintaining that because a hole-in-one in golf is so difficult to achieve, it can never be replicated, whereas we know it is not only repeated often but is frequently not even a newsworthy accomplishment anymore.

The Drake Equation

So how good are the chances that intelligent life exists out there? While most scientists consider life itself a near certainty, they are thinking more along the lines of things like microorganisms and molds rather than advanced civilizations with spaceships. But there are those who consider the prospect of intelligent life—however one cares to define the word *intelligent*—as pretty good. In fact, according to something called the Drake equation, an attempt to estimate the number of extraterrestrial civilizations in our galaxy (devised by Dr. Frank Drake in the 1960s), the chances may be *very good indeed*.

The Drake equation is a complex mathematical formula that takes into account such factors as the rate of formation of stars similar to our own sun (assuming our sun to be the best "type" of star where advanced life is concerned), how many such suns are likely to have planets and what fraction of them are likely to be Earth-like (i.e., liquid water and an atmosphere), and even more important, what tiny number of such planets are likely to develop some form or life, at least on a very basic level. That number—still in the many millions—is then divided by the number of such planets where higher forms of life might develop, which is then divided again by the number of those where intelligent life actually emerges, the percentage of intelligent species who can communicate in a way we could detect, and the lifetime of the communicating civilizations themselves. In the end, even using fairly conservative estimates—and working with only a two hundred billion star galaxy—Drake finally concluded the number of such civilizations in our galaxy alone could be as high as *ten thousand!* Of course, there are those who dispute his numbers, but if he's even close to being right, the fact that he came up with such a staggering number is sobering. In either case, Drake's equation (later championed by the late astronomer Carl Sagan) made science—and religion, for that matter—increasingly open to the prospect that we are not only far from alone, but we may, in fact, be but one of a vast number of planets sprinkled throughout the universe teeming with life.

Overcoming the Technological Hurdle

However, it's not as simple as that. Even if intelligent life does exist, that doesn't automatically assume that such a civilization is necessarily capable of traversing the vast distances between the stars. There is a huge difference between a world capable of building skyscrapers and one capable of producing vehicles that can transit the galaxy with the same ease with which we can cross the Atlantic; it simply doesn't follow that the one makes the other inevitable, and that brings us to our next question: is interstellar travel even *theoretically* possible?

Einstein's theory of relativity seems pretty clear about the fact that nothing of mass can travel faster than the speed of light, and since the distance to even our nearest star is over four light years (about twenty-four *trillion* miles), that makes even the shortest one-way journey between solar systems, utilizing the fastest and most exotic propulsion systems conceivable to us, something that would still take many decades to complete, thereby rendering the prospect of interstellar exploration—at least for us—unfeasible. This presumption, however, works from the premise that we possess a sufficient understanding of the laws of physics to determine what is possible in terms of FTL (faster than light) travel, which truly is a leap of faith. The fact is that we simply don't know enough to determine what is possible—or impossible—in terms of traveling at such speeds (or, more precisely, ways to circumvent Einstein's law without breaking it). The burgeoning field of quantum physics is pushing the boundaries of what we think we know each day, rendering the assumption that we can be definitive about anything increasingly erroneous. Even Albert Einstein had the humility to recognize that his theory of relativity may one day be superseded by new discoveries in physics and science (in much the same way his theories rendered traditional Newtonian physics incomplete);

as such, we would be presumptuous to decide with any degree of certainty that FTL travel is impossible.

The second erroneous presumption science frequently makes is that since *we're* not capable of finding a way around Einstein's pesky little law to achieve FTL speed, *nobody else is either*. Again, this is little more than hubris speaking and is akin to the nineteenth-century assumption that since man had not yet then devised the means of achieving heavier-than-air flight, flying, then, was impossible—a premise the Wright brothers dispatched with considerable ease in 1903. If there are advanced civilizations elsewhere in the universe, it is reasonable to imagine that at least some of them will be as far ahead of us in terms of science and technology as we are ahead of our nineteenth-century counterparts. Certainly, even the most gifted minds of one hundred years ago could not have conceived of transonic flight, laser eye surgery, or the atomic bomb; is the thought of FTL travel the same sort of blind spot in our day? As such, the prospect of interstellar travel, no matter how unlikely it may appear to us from our limited perspective, must be considered at least as plausible as the possibility of advanced civilizations existing among the stars. It simply doesn't make sense that either of them could be possible without *both* of them being equally possible.

This is the premise, then, upon which our exploration of UFOs must be based. To dismiss them outright because of a presumption that life is possible only on this single planet and nowhere else is not an appeal to reason, but an appeal to faith—or, perhaps more accurately, opinion—much as is the position that FTL travel is impossible. Until such a time that we have cracked every secret of the cosmos and pried every molecule of knowledge from it, any statement either affirming or denying the possibility of extraterrestrial intelligence (or its potential technological capabilities) must remain merely a matter of personal opinion.

Why the Empty Skies, Then?

This does bring up an interesting question, though, and that is if Drake's calculations are correct and there may be potentially *thousands* of advanced alien civilizations in existence in our galaxy alone, then why isn't there a virtual smorgasbord of alien vessels from hundreds of different races clogging our skies and generally making a nuisance of themselves?

Of course, there are those who claim that such *is* the case—hence the wide variety of UFO types, shapes, and characteristics that have been observed—but Drake's equation suggests as many as *ten thousand* such space-faring races may be out there! Even if we were only being observed by just 1 percent of them, that's still hundreds of different alien civilizations potentially orbiting our planet at any given time (and that doesn't even take into account the possibility of extremely advanced civilizations visiting us from other *galaxies*).

The first thing to recognize, however, is that Drake did not maintain that all these races had *interstellar* capabilities, but only that they had the ability to *communicate* with us. In fact, they might be just as "earthbound" as we are—regardless of how advanced their technology might prove to be otherwise. Even so, it seems reasonable to assume that at least *a few* of these races—especially the older and more advanced among them—should possess *some* space-faring capability beyond the ability to travel within their own system—thereby rendering the prospect of crowded skies still quite reasonable.

Another point that needs to be taken into account, however, is whether all theses races would *want* to visit us. We often imagine that any space-faring civilization would automatically want to inspect every corner of the cosmos, but we have no evidence that all sentient beings possess the degree of curiosity or desire for exploration that we do. It's not unreasonable to imagine that some may consider us too primitive to bother with and—especially considering our rather remote location in relation to the rest of the galaxy—

too far away to justify the logistical effort getting here would entail. But even then, however, there should still be a *few* races that would find us a worthy subject for study, thereby justifying the likely considerable expenditure in time and energy traveling the immense distances to observe us would require. If such civilizations accounted for just a tiny percentage of the potential number of space-faring races out there, that should still leave many scores or potentially even hundreds of civilizations quite willing and capable of "checking us out."

But even if one is willing to accept at least the possibility that extraterrestrials exist and, further, that they are visiting our planet, the next question—or objection if you prefer—is determining *why* they would do so, especially if we speculate that the galaxy may be home to literally thousands of species equally as interesting as ourselves. To determine that, it will next be necessary to consider the reasons why extraterrestrials would want to come here, for in doing so we may come closer to understanding the motivation behind the things they seem to be doing on our planet.

chapter three

Extraterrestrial Motives
for Visiting Earth

Ever since Kenneth Arnold first saw a formation of brightly colored, crescent-shaped craft flying near Mount Rainier over sixty years ago, the question of what extraterrestrials want from us has haunted mankind. Are they here to conquer us in an effort to colonize Earth and turn us into slave labor or, worse, exterminate us so they might have the earth's rich resources to themselves—an idea so vividly portrayed in movies like *Independence Day* and *War of the Worlds*? Or are they instead benevolent and intent on keeping us from destroying ourselves—as was the theme of the 1951 classic *The Day the Earth Stood Still*? Or, instead, are they looking for an opportunity to reveal themselves and in doing so usher in a new era of cosmic peace and understanding, à la *Close Encounters of the Third Kind*? Or, for that matter, do they simply wish to observe us with the same dispassionate indifference we might exhibit toward beavers in the process of building their dams?

Of course, determining an extraterrestrial civilization's motives for doing anything must, by necessity, be a matter of guesswork. However, I submit that while an alien's physiology may be very different from our own, their inherent sentience should make them more like ourselves than we might imagine. For example, it is likely that many inherent aspects of sentience such as curiosity, intelligence, compassion, and a reverence for life are universal constants, making ETs more "human" than we might expect. Of course, the more negative aspects of sentience such as fear, greed, apathy, and arrogance may also be universal constants as well, but in either case, an extraterrestrial civilization's rationale for moving beyond its own system should be similar to our own, permitting us to make some pretty good guesses about what they might want with us—assuming they can get here in the first place.

The reason for extraterrestrials coming here generally falls into five categories. There may be other motives than the five I list, of course, or even multiple motives may be at work—especially if we are talking about more than a single race here—but these should be a good place to start. Let's examine each in turn to determine how likely—or logical—each rationale might be.

Alien Invaders

When "flying saucers" first entered the collective consciousness in the late 1940s, the assumption that aliens were here to conquer us may not have been so far-fetched as first thought. After all, we had just fought a world war and were in the midst of the Cold War with an opponent as bristling with nuclear weapons as we were, so extraterrestrials could easily be seen as simply the next threat in line. In fact, the possibility that UFOs may have posed a very real military threat was the very reason the Air Force established Project Sign in 1948—precisely to ascertain just how dangerous these "flying disks" might be.

This belief that aliens possibly meant us harm remained a major element of the national mindset throughout the early years of the UFO phenomenon, evolving into a major theme of science-fiction movies throughout the 1950s and 1960s. It wasn't until these images were eventually replaced by more benign aliens in the 1970s and

'80s via such movies as *Close Encounters of the Third Kind* and *E.T.* that extraterrestrials began to shed their menacing persona, but even then the thought that at least some of them may still pose a threat remains an integral part of the human mindset to this day, as evidenced by other, more recent films such as *Independence Day* and M. Night Shyamalan's *Signs*. It appears that despite forty years of *Star Trek*—which often portrays aliens as benevolent—humanity continues to harbor more than a small degree of suspicion, fear, and even overt hostility toward extraterrestrials, as is consistent with humanity's general distrust of anything considered alien, mysterious, or foreign in general.

Of course, this fear isn't entirely groundless, especially when one considers the highly advanced technology a space-faring race would likely have at its disposal. When we consider the level of destruction we are capable of committing at our current "primitive" level of development, the thought of what a race even a couple of centuries ahead of us might be capable of is sobering to consider.

Fortunately, however, UFOs do not appear to be so inclined to turn their "blasters" on us, at least from all outward appearances. If extraterrestrials are here at all, it is logical to imagine they have been here for some time (perhaps centuries, if some ancient texts are to be taken seriously) and, as such, would have had ample opportunity to dispose of us at any point had conquering the planet been their intent. In fact, were they determined to scour the planet clean of our presence (or, at the very least, enslave us), it makes no sense that they wouldn't have done it long before we developed the technology (i.e., nuclear weapons, nerve agents, lasers, missiles) to offer at least token resistance. As such, the main reason we can discount the evil-alien scenario is because we're still here.

Of course, it's possible that more malevolent alien races simply haven't arrived yet, so we can't entirely discount the possibility of one day having to do battle with visitors from the stars, but this still seems unlikely to me for two reasons: first, it is my contention that for an advanced civilization to reach the levels of technology

necessary to achieve interstellar flight, it would need to be emotionally, psychologically, and spiritually evolved enough to handle
that technology (i.e., wise enough not to turn it on themselves or
their neighbors), making it far less likely that they would use that
technology for conquest. Of course, it would be equally presumptuous to decide that there are therefore no warlike or aggressive
races at all, but I suspect that if there are, they are either still at a
comparatively primitive level of development—and as such have a
good chance of destroying themselves long before they either reach
us or achieve the pinnacle of technological sophistication to be
truly dangerous—or they are possibly being restrained in some way
by other, more spiritually developed and technologically advanced
races (a possibility we will consider in more detail in a moment).

The second problem with the alien invasion scenario is in
understanding an alien civilization's motive in attacking us. Colonization is usually considered the most likely rationale, especially
if habitable planets like Earth are rare, or they might see Earth as a
source of valuable resources to be harvested or mined. Both theories
fail the test of logic, however, when considered from the standpoint
of practicality. First, the likelihood that any alien being could survive on our planet with its unique mix of temperature, air pressure,
gravity, and oxygen is extremely doubtful. If an alien race's home
planet is even slightly different from our own in terms of atmosphere and radiation levels, for example, the conditions that make
life possible for us might well prove lethal to them. Unless they had
an extremely tough and highly adaptable metabolism or possessed
the technology to transform our planet to make it more like their
home world (known as terraforming, a process that can take centuries), colonization would likely prove impractical.

Then there's the problem of Earth's microorganisms to contend
with. Even if all multicellular life was eradicated from the face of
the planet as part of an extraterrestrial colonization effort, it would
be almost impossible to ensure that all microbial life could be
entirely eliminated. Some bacteria and viruses would undoubtedly

survive to play havoc with an alien immune system, again making living on our planet potentially lethal. Unless they had an immune system that could handle any foreign microbe or destroyed all life to the microscopic level (thereby rendering Earth entirely sterile and so negating its value as a source of colonization, one would think), it is doubtful any alien species could survive long on our planet—much less thrive.

As for harvesting the earth's resources, this too seems like a lot of trouble to go through for minimal gain. The earth is not unique in its chemical composition; there are literally billions of ore-rich planets sprinkled throughout the galaxy, most of them probably closer to the alien race's home world than our own and, best of all, lifeless. It would be far easier, and probably more cost-effective and less problematic, to simply find a large, dead asteroid somewhere and cut it into smaller pieces that could be easily transferred to their home world if rare Earth metals were truly what they are after. Conquering Earth (and potentially destroying one of the most vibrant ecosystems in the galaxy at the same time) seems like a high price to pay for what could only be considered mere ore collecting.

Finally, as I suggested earlier, while I suppose it's possible there could be races out there who simply enjoy destroying things (or perhaps consider humans fair game for sporting events, as suggested in the film *Predator*), I believe such an aggressive race would most likely destroy itself—probably in a quest for power, territory, or wealth—long before turning its vast arsenal upon us. And even if it did somehow survive its own tendency toward violence, there is the question of how other equally advanced—or even superior—races would respond to their wanton destructiveness. Is it possible there are "guardian" races out there who take responsibility for our protection from less enlightened races (and who possess the means to successfully do so)? I'd imagine if we have been a source of study by other alien races for millennia, it's likely we've acquired a sort of "protected species" status by now, keeping us safe for future study.

Earth as a Threat

A second rationale for alien interference is more defensive than offensive in nature: extraterrestrials may consider us a potential threat and so are intent on stopping us before we become a danger to them (assuming we aren't already). In essence, extraterrestrials may be very concerned about our nuclear arsenals and growing space-faring capabilities, but being too enlightened to use force to stop us, have to resort to more benign methods of getting us to behave ourselves.

This is a common notion among many ufologists and New Agers, but it too fails to pass the test of logic. Consider that any race capable of traveling between the stars already possesses a degree of technology many centuries or even thousands of years ahead of our own. If that is the case, one would imagine that would make us no more dangerous to them than a Stone Age tribe armed with blow-guns would be to a modern U.S. Army battalion. Undoubtedly, they may have concerns about our nuclear arsenals (much as our army battalion may be concerned about a booming poison-tipped arrow trade flourishing among the natives), but in terms of us posing a direct threat to their world dozens or even hundreds of light years away, I suspect they have little to worry about.

But who's to say that they may not be worried about a time in the future when we might genuinely pose some sort of legitimate threat, especially once we acquire the same interstellar capabilities and learn to harness many of the same energy sources they do? While that's a possibility, consider that in the time it takes us to develop a full-blown interstellar capability—say two hundred years—any alien civilization studying us today will also have continued to advance as well, keeping us always well behind them in terms of technological equivalency. In effect, we would always be playing a game of galactic catch-up, with our competition consistently remaining several generations ahead of us in terms of capability and, as such, perpetually rendering us insignificant as a threat.

Genetic Manipulation and Seeding

One of the more controversial theories as to why aliens may be interested in us has more to do with our physiology than anything else; in other words, it's our bodies they want, not our planet. This hypothesis works in two ways: either we are an ongoing genetic experiment they began hundreds of thousands of years ago and continue today—effectively making *Homo sapiens* the byproduct of alien seeding experiments (which they continue to "tweak" to this day in an effort to further our evolution as a species), or ETs are trying to splice their DNA into our own—thereby creating a race of hybrid human/aliens—in an effort to save their own race from extinction. Let's look at both ideas for a moment to determine how plausible either of them are from the standpoint of logic.

The rationale behind the first concept—let's call it the *seeding hypothesis*—appears to be part of a larger alien agenda designed to directly introduce advanced life forms onto suitable planets throughout the galaxy. The idea here is to give evolution a "kick start" by finding suitable life forms—in our case, advanced primates—and then introducing genetic enhancements incrementally over thousands of years in an effort to advance the species to a point at which higher intelligence becomes possible. This would make *Homo sapiens*, then, a "designer species" brought into existence not through the natural process of evolution but through the use of some sort of exotic alien technology. This supposedly explains why sentient life seemed to appear so suddenly on our planet a mere one hundred thousand years ago after hundreds of millions of years of evolution failed to do the trick.

The reason behind the second hypothesis—let's call it the *eugenics hypothesis*—is less clear but seems to have something to do with extraterrestrials protecting themselves from extinction, which they do by abducting people and performing all sorts of bizarre medical procedures on them. What exactly these procedures are designed to do is not certain, but it is thought that the extraterrestrials either extract samples of human DNA from their victims that are then taken back to their planet and spliced back into their own species, thereby restoring it to genetic health; or they are injecting their own DNA into our genomes in an attempt to produce a sort of "hybrid" race of extraterrestrial humans, thereby ensuring their continued survival—at least in a hybrid form. In both scenarios, human beings are being used essentially as guinea pigs, apparently against their will and frequently even without their knowledge, as part of a brutal exercise in genetic manipulation. This is what supposedly explains the large number of alien abduction reports—by some estimates, in the tens of thousands worldwide over the last fifty years.

While both theories would—and frequently do—make great storylines for sci-fi adventures, from a purely scientific standpoint there are a number of problems inherent to both of them. First, the idea that it would be possible—even using the most advanced technology imaginable—to merge the genetic material of two entirely unrelated species flies in the face of everything we understand about the physical sciences. Despite how physiologically similar we might be to another species (and by all accounts we appear to be *very* different from the "grays" [7] of UFO lore), the idea that an alien species could splice their DNA with ours in an effort to either revitalize their own race or alter ours is highly unlikely. There would simply be too many variables in play and the difference in sequencing and genetic compatibility would undoubtedly be profound. (Plus, wouldn't such an influx of alien genes show up in medical scans, especially now that we have perfected the technology to read a person's unique DNA fingerprint?)

As far as the seeding hypothesis goes, not only does it suffer from many of the same difficulties (i.e., introducing alien DNA into a primate in an effort to create a human), but it has the additional problem of not being apparent in the fossil record. Had such a series of alterations been attempted on our primate ancestors, we

---

7.   The nickname given to the small, hairless, gray-skinned aliens usually mentioned in most abduction accounts.

should see a number of sudden, inexplicable advances in the development of our species rather than the comparatively slow progression over millions of years that has been noted by anthropologists. Further, and perhaps even more relevant, what alien race possesses the longevity to conduct a seeding experiment over a period of tens or even hundreds of thousands of years? It seems reasonable to assume that such a civilization would have either died out, been destroyed, or otherwise vanished long before they had the chance to realize the fruits of their labors.

As such, it seems unlikely that ETs are here to genetically experiment on us, although I suppose the idea isn't entirely out of the question; if they look at us the same way we might look at lab rats, playing with our genetic makeup might be of interest to them. The problem is that if that were their game, why perform their experiments on abductees and then release them with suppressed memories intact (an issue we will look at in more detail later), thereby dramatically improving the chances of being found out? It would make more sense to simply abduct a few hundred worthy subjects and keep them isolated in a controlled environment (the mothership perhaps?) where the results could be carefully monitored and secrecy ensured. With literally thousands of people reported missing each year in this country alone—and with many never being seen again—I suspect we would never notice if a few hundred of our fellow citizens vanished as part of an alien genetics experiment.

And finally, what would other alien races think of these little eugenics experiments? Might they not consider them to be somewhat outside both the letter and spirit of noninterference and so be prompted to take action? If there are guardian races watching over us, I should think they would interpret forced genetic experimentation to be every bit as destructive as an invasion and as likely to result in much the same response.

Messengers from the Stars

To many people, another increasingly appealing and popular idea about why aliens might be here, one related to the "Earth as a threat" scenario, is that extraterrestrials may not be worried about themselves personally but instead possess a sort of cosmic maternal instinct that makes them feel compelled to save us from destroying ourselves, either militarily or environmentally. In fact, this is one of the favorite extraterrestrial "gospels" being touted by some ufologists and New Agers today, who imagine extraterrestrials to not only be our friends but in many ways our saviors, thereby replacing our traditional deities with benevolent spacemen.

While I admit to finding this a far more appealing hypothesis than alien invaders and genetic manipulators, it too suffers from many of the problems the conquering-aliens scenario does: namely, if their intention is to save us from ourselves, why haven't they done so by now? Are they waiting for things to get worse, and if so, why? It seems that if they are interstellar missionaries, they need to make their message known now, not decades from now when there may be nothing left to rescue. Even Christian missionaries sent to save the "heathens" from eternal judgment didn't travel to darkest Africa and then wait years before starting the work of proselytizing; they were usually building churches and converting natives the day they arrived. Would we expect anything different from an alien race of saviors?

Some have suggested that extraterrestrials *have* been trying to save us for centuries but have been doing so in more subtle, less intrusive ways. These people point to religion as one vehicle they may have used in an attempt to bring enlightenment (the "Jesus was a spaceman" theory), or that they may entrust certain individuals to get their message out through books and the media, thereby reducing the chance of panic or resistance if their agenda were more obvious. In this way, then, the extraterrestrials can influence our culture for the better without having to reveal themselves.

This argument again suffers from a few flaws, however. First, religion has done little to unify the planet or move it toward enlightenment, so introducing religion to humanity is a poor means of saving it from itself. It might make sense if extraterrestrials had introduced a single, unifying religion designed to supersede all others a thousand years ago, but the very multitude and cross-purposes of the various faiths argues against religion being an alien invention. Clearly, whether used for good or bad—and it is capable of being used for either—religion is a man-made invention designed to make sense of the universe, not save man from himself.

Second, introducing extraterrestrial concepts of peace and environmental responsibility through human intermediaries also appears to be a weak approach. Most writers and spokespeople for these movements—while they have their audiences and do influence people to some degree—constitute only a tiny percentage of the populace and have a very limited impact on national or public policy. Using New Age writers to get the word out strikes me as the equivalent of placing a few billboards around the country beseeching people to behave themselves, and about as likely to be effective. If extraterrestrials are intent on saving us from our own destructive and selfish tendencies, changing one mind at a time is a dangerously slow way to go about it.

Then there is the question as to what extent an alien culture— especially an enlightened one intent on saving us from destruction—is ethically willing to go to introduce its gospel of peace. In other words, in order to save us from our own shortsightedness and foolishness, wouldn't it necessitate destroying our current culture to do so?[8] Earth is a unique social system that any sufficiently enlightened race should know better than to tamper with lest they create more problems than they solve. Plus, how do they introduce themselves without creating panic on a worldwide scale, and what of

---

8.   It is also uncertain how other alien races in the area would respond to our helpful neighbors' good intentions. Is it possible that guardian races aren't just protecting us from our more malevolent neighbors, but from our more benevolent ones as well?

those cultures that refuse to embrace their social gospel? Obviously the work of planetary savior is far more problematic than many may appreciate.

Scientific Observation

That, then, leaves the only other rationale for their presence, and that is that extraterrestrials are here to study us, which is the position I believe makes the most sense—at least from the standpoint of science. If we assume that extraterrestrials are as curious about what lies among the stars as we are, it only makes sense that once they procured the means to expand beyond their own systems, they would use that ability to study other worlds—precisely as we will do once we acquire a similar capability. I'd imagine that for most sentient races, the desire to learn more than what is possible from the confines of a home planet would be a powerful inducement to strike out across the cosmos.

And not just a single race either; if Drake's equation is even close to correct, we can surmise that there may be hundreds or even thousands of space-faring civilizations in our galaxy crisscrossing the vast distances on voyages of discovery, and that at least a few of them may be close enough to make an excursion to our little corner of the galactic arm worthwhile.

The objection—expressed by some—that asks why we would be of interest to such an advanced race is a non-starter; any sentient race, regardless of how primitive it was, would likely be of tremendous interest to another more advanced race, if only to see how it compares to their own and in contributing to their understanding of how various independent sentient cultures develop. Just as anthropologists will spend years studying primitive cultures on our own planet, extraterrestrials may find us equally as fascinating; in fact, I can't imagine how the ET equivalent of an anthropologist, biologist, sociologist, or historian could resist the opportunity to study a developing civilization such as ours firsthand, especially if such civilizations are relatively rare to begin with.

Of course, it's possible that some races may not care what lies beyond their own planet, but I personally find such a premise difficult to believe. One of the hallmarks of higher intelligence appears to be curiosity, which is also the mechanism that powers all scientific discovery and advancement. As such, it seems self-evident that for a civilization to evolve to the point of being able to travel between the stars, it would have to be curious—at least to some degree. I simply don't see how it could grow in knowledge otherwise.

Additionally, exploring the universe would be more than simply an exercise in curiosity but may also be an element of an alien race's own means of self-preservation. For example, it would be helpful to know what other races are out there and which of them might harbor certain hostile tendencies before waiting for them to suddenly appear, at which point it may be too late to defend oneself. I realize I stated earlier there was only a minimal chance that an extraterrestrial race would be hostile, and I maintain that to be the case still; however, that doesn't preclude the possibility that there aren't at least a few interstellar civilizations out there—probably in their earliest stages of development—that may work from a more primitive perspective or possess such a strong martial history that the use of force may be a part of their repertoire. If so, I suspect such races to be the exception rather than the rule, but they would still need to be accounted for and, if necessary, defended against, further necessitating that a thorough exploration of the galaxy be undertaken.

Conclusions

Of course, determining a potential motive for other advanced races to visit is one thing, but it hardly stands to follow that doing so proves that they are here. I have only demonstrated that since there is a reasonable chance that advanced civilizations may exist, they would have a number of good reasons for wanting to come here—presuming they have found a way to overcome the technological hurdles traveling among the stars would entail. In other words, the *theoretical* case for extraterrestrial visitation has been laid, if not the practical case for it. And that, of course, is light years away from proving that UFOs are real or, if they are, that they are of extraterrestrial origin.

Finally, while the existence of extraterrestrial life—and most specifically intelligent, space-faring civilizations—remains to some degree an article of faith, it is not an appeal to blind faith, nor is it scientifically untenable. While the prospect has been sensationalized over the years and is frequently lost in a maelstrom of nonsense, the objective observer should be able to proceed with the knowledge that, at a minimum, they are not delving into a fantasy world when considering the issue, but are on reasonably solid scientific ground.

chapter four

Alternative UFO Theories

Up to now we have worked from the premise that those mysterious objects we call UFOs are highly sophisticated and remarkably complex machines produced by alien civilizations hundreds or perhaps even thousands of light years away. However, what if we are being premature in this assumption? After all, even if we can make a good case for the likelihood of advanced alien life existing on other planets, that doesn't automatically demonstrate that the UFOs we see in our skies are vessels from those planets. In fact, it doesn't necessarily demand they even be physical objects at all. However, if they're not extraterrestrial or physical objects of some kind, what else might they be?

A number of non-extraterrestrial hypotheses as to what these mysterious craft might be have been suggested over the years, some of which are very intriguing. As such, and in the spirit of making this study as thorough as possible, let's examine some of these frequently controversial and highly speculative theories out there. Of course, some may argue that looking at the more exotic explanations for UFOs might be an unnecessary tangent to our purpose, but I believe it's important to examine every possibility, no matter how unlikely it may be. After all, we never know what we might find once we are willing to open our minds, and this subject is nothing if not an opportunity to think outside the normal boundaries of science.

Alternative UFO hypotheses generally fall into two categories: terrestrial and metaphysical. With terrestrial hypotheses, the physical nature of UFOs is not in question but only their points of origin, making them still akin to the extraterrestrial hypothesis in the respect that UFOs remain "real" objects, the difference being that they are not "spaceships" from another planet but are instead highly sophisticated craft being operated by hidden or "lost" civilizations here on Earth. Other theories that fall under the terrestrial venue are that UFOs may be evidence of human time travel—UFOs being, in essence, the devices used to make the journey from the future—or that they are some as yet undiscovered "space" animals of some kind that, due to their unique flight characteristics, are mistaken for extraterrestrial craft.

Metaphysical theories, in contrast, take a different approach entirely. They consider the possibility that UFOs are not solid or "real" objects at all, but either the manifestation of intradimensional beings or the product of purposely directed psychic energy that takes on the appearance of form while remaining fully immaterial. In essence, metaphysical UFOs are more form than substance, though they can often appear extremely "solid" to our senses.

Although each of these theories has its proponents, it's fair to say that none of them enjoy the degree of popular support the extraterrestrial hypothesis does—usually for good reason: they are too speculative or dependent upon processes we know nothing about to make them particularly attractive. They are still worthy of examination, however, if only in an effort to broaden our perspectives on the subject and give us food for thought.

Alternative Hypothesis # 1: UFOs are terrestrial craft being operated by a hidden civilization here on Earth

Some ufologists have suggested that we don't need to look to the stars to find the source of these mysterious objects in the skies (and, sometimes, under the water) but need look no further than our own planet. In other words, UFOs are not extraterrestrial at all, but simply evidence of an unknown and largely mysterious Earth-borne civilization that is so advanced that we simply presume it to be alien.

This idea at first suggests that UFOs are "secret" or experimental vehicles being operated by our own—or a foreign—government, but that's not what is usually meant by this hypothesis. Nor are we talking about the possibility that extraterrestrials may maintain bases at the bottom of the world's oceans or inside extinct volcanoes, thereby explaining their frequent appearance over water and mountain ranges. Instead, what this theory suggests is that UFOs are machines that are being operated from hidden bases here on Earth by a highly advanced and fully terrestrial but "hidden" civilization that flourishes somewhere just beyond our means to detect it.

The "hidden civilization" theory falls into one of two camps, the first of which I have dubbed the *Atlantis scenario* and the second, the *Abyss scenario*. In the former, these beings are fully human and indistinguishable from ourselves but live on areas of the planet inaccessible to us, such as the bottom of the sea or within subterranean caverns; in the later scenario, these beings are nonhuman but sentient creatures native to this planet that evolved on Earth alongside (and apparently unbeknownst) to ourselves in places generally inaccessible to us—again, like the sea floor or underground. While both are admittedly fantastic notions, neither is necessarily any more remarkable than the idea that visitors from beyond the stars may be hiding in bases here on Earth, so we should be willing to examine each possibility with equal seriousness.

The Atlantis scenario has certain strengths that make it appealing. For example, a "parallel civilization" existing alongside our own would not only account for why some saucer occupants appear completely human but why they are sometimes even capable of interacting with witnesses on an intimate level. Being fully human would also permit them to observe us firsthand as well as solve the cross-contamination problem so destructive with inter-species contact. Some have even suggested that such a civilization may be the actual remnants of Atlantis itself, which was driven underground (or underwater) thousands of years ago and remains there today, where it continues to develop its extraordinary technology beneath our very noses. Such a civilization may also be behind many of the ancient traditions of visitors from the heavens so popular within many cultures around the world, suggesting that it may have been flourishing on our planet for many centuries.

However, there are a few problems with this scenario. The biggest, of course, is in understanding how a parallel civilization could exist on this planet without our detecting it—especially with the technology available to us today. Clearly, the only place such would be even potentially possible would be the bottom of the sea or in some deep subterranean environment, but how would such a civilization be able to create and maintain its society from within the confines of either environment? Any civilization that once existed on the surface before being driven into a purely aquatic environment, for example, would need to overcome the staggering engineering challenges building underwater structures capable of maintaining such a civilization would entail. Not only would the challenges of building structures capable of withstanding the intense water pressures encountered at the bottom of even a shallow sea be considerable—much less miles down where their anonymity would be more readily assured—but how does this society survive without sunlight in the deepest parts of the ocean or within the bowels of the earth? Even if it might be argued that such an advanced civilization may have developed the technology to offset these problems (i.e., fiber-optic technology to transfer light to the ocean depths, geothermal energy sources, aqualungs to convert water into breathable air, and the like), that doesn't tell us how this civilization was capable of surviving before such technologies had been perfected. Obviously, they would have needed to possess such technology before going "underground" (so to speak), but then if they did possess such advanced technology tens of thousands of years ago—technologies that we ourselves have yet to perfect today—then why leave the surface at all?

Finally, even if we could account for all these factors, why would this civilization continue to remain hidden today? If they initially hid to protect themselves from something or "someone" (and whoever that might be would have needed to possess an even greater degree of technology than our "Atlanteans" in order to pose a credible threat), we can only surmise that the danger has since passed and they can return safely to the surface. Of course, it's possible that they are hesitant to do so because they are afraid of *us* and our modern weapons and so remain hidden for their own protection, but that makes even less sense: if their technology is considerably more advanced than our own—as seems to be the case—they appear capable of easily defeating us "surface dwellers," so why not simply use that technology to reclaim the surface from which they were originally driven? I suppose they could be intensely xenophobic or are so spiritually evolved that they no longer possess the aggressiveness necessary to even consider such a thing, but neither possibility sounds particularly believable: surely they would be aware that we possess the means to alter the earth's climate—including our oceans—in major and unpredictable ways, thereby potentially threatening their own survival in the process. I should think that fact alone would bring them to the surface, leaving the entire hypothesis with more questions than answers.

The other hypothesis—that of the parallel evolved, nonhuman race of fully aquatic, sentient beings (the *Abyss* scenario[9])— would account for how a civilization could exist at the bottom of

---

9. Named in honor of the excellent 1989 film that captured this concept perfectly.

the ocean (they evolved in water so the great pressures wouldn't be a problem), but it leaves us with a number of other questions to ponder. For example, how could beings who have never lived in a non-aquatic environment have made vital discoveries like fire—an indispensable element without which metallurgy and most other forms of manufacturing would be impossible—from the bottom of the sea? Additionally, if fully adapted to an aquatic environment, shouldn't they have "fish-like" characteristics (webbed hands and gills, for example) and their vessels be filled with ocean water in the same way our submarines are filled with air? Yet rarely has anyone reported aliens as being even remotely aquatic in nature or described their vessels as being essentially flying aquariums. Further, while it is true that areas of the oceans remain largely unexplored and mostly inaccessible to us at our present level of technology, it's difficult to imagine that a marine strain of human could have evolved without leaving some trace of itself in the fossil record in the process—much less develop a full-fledged aquatic civilization without our having stumbled across it at some point.

While I'm the first to admit there may be many mysteries lurking on our planet waiting to reveal themselves, I find it more difficult to accept the idea that there is a hidden civilization flourishing at the bottom of our oceans or beneath the surface of our planet than I do that extraterrestrials might have hidden bases here on Earth. They, at least, would already possess the technology to make such a scenario at least feasible and would have a rationale for remaining hidden—something neither our Atlantean nor aquatic colleagues would possess—keeping both those theories, in my opinion, firmly anchored in the realm of pure speculation.

Alternative Hypothesis # 2: UFOs are vehicles used by our future descendents to travel back in time

Another idea that is becoming increasingly popular with many in the UFO community is that what we call UFOs are not craft from another planet, but instead are vehicles from *another time*. In effect, they are time machines built by our progeny hundreds—or potentially even thousands—of years in the future, who are using them to come back and study us in much the same way we might go back in time to study cavepeople were we to one day acquire a similar time-travel capability. As such, those aliens that appear human, or almost human, look that way because they *are* human (or, at least, more fully evolved humans[10]).

Problems with this theory are twofold: aside from the fact that it is debatable whether time travel is even theoretically possible is the question of whether it would be practical. For example, if it were possible to travel through time (one can only imagine the energy requirements required to punch even a tiny hole in time, much less one large enough to bring an entire ship through such a rift), the most immediate problem is how potentially destructive such an ability might prove to be to both our present and future timelines. In other words, what would happen if one of our time-traveling descendents encountered one of his or her own ancestors and accidentally killed this ancestor—a paradox that has been bandied about by first-year philosophy students for a century? Time travel is chock-full of paradoxes like this, which is what makes it such a popular element of science fiction and leads me to wonder if its acceptance by some people isn't simply another manifestation of our common cultural affinity for time-travel mythologies.

A second problem the time-travel hypothesis brings up is how a person from the future would be able to survive in our time, much

---

10. This hypothesis has also been used to explain the appearance of the "grays"—those small, frail-looking aliens, usually recounted in abduction encounters, who appear almost human but lack apparent ears and noses—as examples of what humans will one day evolve into hundreds of thousands or even millions of years in the future.

less interact with us in any meaningful way. For example, were we to travel back to 50,000 BCE, how would we get around in such a primitive and rugged world? Once we left the security of our ship, we would be at the mercy of the elements, just as our descendents would be were they to arrive in our era. We humans are products of our environments and as such would undoubtedly find it extremely difficult to adjust to another world very different from our own. Unless we remained confined to our time "pod" and just observed from a safe distance (thereby begging the question of why even bother to travel through time in the first place if there's not much we could do once we got there), I should think we would have a very rough time of things.

Another problem is more physiological than practical. For example, how would our modern immune systems handle the primitive bacterial strains that were around fifty thousand years ago? Our ability to successfully fight off infection is an ongoing battle being continually waged between emerging new strains of microorganisms and the ability of our immune systems to constantly adapt to each new mutation as it emerges. However, our bodies are used to fighting modern strains of bacteria and viruses; microorganisms from the distant past—so far removed from their modern counterparts—might easily overwhelm our immune systems, with unfortunate results. In effect, a bug our Neanderthal ancestors might have been able to shrug off with hardly a sniffle might prove fatal to us, while our primitive subjects may be unable to adapt to whatever pathogens we might introduce from our time into their environment, potentially creating a plague that could well wipe them off the face of the earth. (Of course, then there would be no future humans to travel back in time, rendering the entire issue one huge contradiction in any event. There's that paradox thing again.)

It's conceivable that some of these problems might be overcome with adequate preparation and a high degree of technology, but even then it still strikes me as self-evident that interjecting oneself into the distant past couldn't be anything other than dangerous to us and to them—both physically and in terms of time-altering paradoxes. As such, the time-travel theory, while intriguing, must remain purely speculative and so is unlikely to provide us with any useful information about the nature of UFOs—at least until our time-traveling descendents decide to make themselves known to us.

Alternative Hypothesis # 3:
UFOs are some sort of exotic "space animal"

Certainly one of the more unusual theories about the nature of UFOs is that they are not, in actuality, mechanical devices at all, but are instead terrestrial creatures that live in space—or, at least, reside in the highest reaches of our atmosphere—where they flourish completely undetectable except under ideal circumstances. This would explain their remarkable maneuvering ability (sometimes described as "undulating," "gliding," or "fluid," much like a stingray) and general invisibility, as well as why they rarely appear on radar scopes. That they appear at all could be explained through some sort of bioluminescence—a feature shared by some deep-sea fish—that allows them to glow with an almost ethereal sheen when conditions are right (perhaps activated when they descend into lower levels of the atmosphere, thereby bringing them into our awareness).

Obviously, there are several problems with this theory. First, since UFOs are frequently reported to achieve supersonic speeds and to be capable of undertaking maneuvers our fastest jet fighters are incapable of matching, we have to wonder how such a creature could achieve such remarkable feats of aeronautics. Additionally, we would have to ponder why it appears in so many different shapes and sizes—from nearly a mile in diameter (as some have reported) to no larger than a basketball—and why it exhibits so many different lighting characteristics and colors. But perhaps the biggest problem with this theory has to do with the sheer physiology of such an animal. If this is a biological creature, it is difficult to imagine how it might survive in the upper reaches of the subzero, oxygen-deprived cold of the stratosphere, where temperatures can reach -200°F and there is not enough oxygen to keep a candle flame lit. Additionally, how does the creature remain airborne in such a thin atmosphere, what would it eat, how would it survive the dangerously high levels of cosmic radiation evident at those altitudes, and how could such an animal exist for perhaps millions of years without leaving some trace of itself in the fossil record? (What happens when it dies, for instance? Wouldn't it fall to Earth?)

Clearly, if such an animal existed, it would possess a physiology so alien to anything we have encountered before that it would be, for all intents and purposes, extraterrestrial in both nature and makeup. Unless proponents of such a theory can come up with some means by which such an organism could exist in what could only be considered a sterile environment, the space-animal hypothesis must remain firmly entrenched in the realm of fantasy rather than anything approaching a real explanation for UFOs.

Alternative Hypothesis # 4: UFOs are vehicles being operated by intradimensional beings

Another interesting but ultimately unprovable hypothesis is that what we call extraterrestrials are not beings from another planet, but beings from another dimension who have the capacity to enter our dimension at will. This supposedly explains how they can both appear and disappear with such speed without leaving traces of themselves, as well as why they can do the many remarkable feats they are supposedly capable of performing. Some people have even suggested that there may be a multitude of intradimensional races of sentient beings, each capable of making the trip between dimensions, thereby explaining the vast array of different vehicles and aliens often reported.

The primary difficulty with this theory, however, is that while the existence of multiple dimensions is a foundational principle of quantum physics, it is difficult to understand the process by which one of these parallel dimensions might be left and another entered without fundamentally altering the nature of the beings making the shift. In other words, if there are multiple dimensions (or, as some have taken to calling them, parallel universes) in existence—each with their own sentient beings—then we might imagine that each would operate according to its own unique set of physics and physiology, making the journey from one realm to another problematic and, potentially, even lethal. It's also not clear why these entities would require the use of a vessel to make this jump rather than simply accessing a "portal" or other equally fantastic "intradimensional doorway" of some kind to move between realms. (And, of course, it doesn't even come close to asking why they would even want to do so in the first place.) Clearly, the entire premise, while occasionally suggested by some in the UFO community, doesn't appear to be well thought out or—for all we know—even theoretically possible. Still, it remains an intriguing hypothesis that may make more sense in the future as we come to better understand the nature of matter and energy. For now, however, it is something better left on the "back burner" in terms of understanding the UFO phenomenon, at least until our knowledge of quantum mechanics and the nature of reality increases dramatically.

Alternative Hypothesis # 5: UFOs are nonphysical manifestations of energy

This theory works from the premise that UFOs are not physical things but are instead very solid looking *manifestations* of energy. In essence, they are things that, even though they may appear physical, are in fact entirely devoid of mass (although, perhaps, not energy).

This idea works in one of two ways. The first is related to the interdimensional-being theory—but instead of there being a race of sentient beings from a parallel universe visiting us, pure manifestations of perhaps intelligently controlled but entirely nonphysical collections of energy are doing the visiting. This would seem to explain why UFOs are occasionally seen not only to appear and disappear so suddenly and perform the sort of maneuvers they do, but even why they sometimes appear to change shape as some observers claim to have witnessed. Obviously, such capabilities would only be possible if UFOs are not solid objects and, as such, are not subjected to the laws of physics as physical matter is.

The second way this idea works is that UFOs are not interdimensional manifestations of energy, but instead are manifestations of human consciousness designed to demonstrate the creative power of thought. This idea basically works along the line that there are people—perhaps highly evolved beings who live among us unawares—who are capable of bringing "things" into manifestation for short periods of time in much the same way that a holographic projector can make nonphysical images appear in three-dimensional space. Why they would do this is uncertain, of course; perhaps such displays are consciousness-expanding demonstrations designed to open humanity up to the possibilities of directed thought as well as introduce us to an entirely new realm of existence (or, in this case, nonexistence). In any case, it is in their being nonphysical in nature (i.e., not possessing mass) that they are able to achieve the astonishing feats of maneuverability and speed they have been observed performing, as well as explain why UFOs don't appear on radar or otherwise leave any evidence of their presence. Of course, in being nonphysical objects, it suggests that they are imaginary, but that is not the case. Instead, such manifestations are more akin to "ghosts"—disassociated energy that takes on the appearance of form without actually becoming a solid object—created and sustained entirely through the sheer will of their creator. And, like ghosts, they are capable of being caught on film before fading back into the ether from which they came.

Obviously, this hypothesis is a purely metaphysical explanation for what UFOs may be and, as such, needs to be understood in that context. However, despite bordering on the mystical and so existing outside of our capacity to study it, it must at least be considered as a possibility—especially in a universe that seems to be brimming with mystery. For our purposes, however, it is a concept better left alone, at least until such a time as we can begin to grasp the principles that may be involved in turning thought into matter, if indeed such a thing is even possible.

Conclusions

So where does all this leave us? If seems that if UFOs are real, the odds of them being something other than extraterrestrial appear slim. Hidden civilizations, time travelers, intradimensional beings, and even bioluminescent space creatures seem to be among the more complex options to consider, leading us back to our original and simpler option, which is that UFOs *are exactly what they appear to be*: extraterrestrial machines that have somehow mastered the ability to traverse the vast distances of space. The wide range of UFO configurations, then, would suggest that Earth is being studied by a number of different races—only a few of which apparently choose to interact with us—or that there are just a few races that have a vast array of different craft at their disposal.

Of course, demonstrating something to be possible does not make it factual. There are those who, despite these arguments, continue to insist that extraterrestrials do not populate our skies now, nor have they ever done so, maintaining instead that all accounts of UFOs are the result of hoaxing, the misidentification of some natural or man-made object, or simple delusions. So do the skeptics have a case? After all, the prospect of extraterrestrial visitors *is* an extraordinary claim, so it's important we look at the skeptics' arguments in an effort to determine how well they, too, stand up to logic.

chapter five

The Case Against Extraterrestrials

The question of whether extraterrestrials exist is an easy one for most skeptics: they do not, and all reports of them are either the product of hoaxes, self-delusion, media-driven mass hysteria, or simple misidentification of natural or man-made aerial phenomena. Case closed.

Of course, considering humanity's propensity toward superstition and our ability to be deceived by our own senses under the proper conditions, this is not an entirely unreasonable premise. People *do* make mistakes about what they see and are often so wedded to what they want to believe to be true that they sometimes unwittingly manufacture the "evidence" to support it. As such, the possibility that UFOs are nothing more—or less—than evidence of simple human error—or, on occasion, mischief—must be carefully weighed when examining the subject.

To that end, let's look at the most common natural and man-made explanations offered to explain away UFOs, in order to see not only how plausible they are but also to help us appreciate how easily an honest and sincere person—and even "professional" observers—can be fooled by what their eyes tell them. Only by understanding how something as seemingly innocuous as the planet Venus could be mistaken for a UFO can we even begin to differentiate fact from fiction and so explore the issue of extraterrestrial visitation in a balanced and objective way.

But before we start, it's first important we consider not only the *observed* phenomena but the *observer* of the phenomena—for it is only in examining the human factor that we can begin to understand why people believe the things they do. Hopefully, in doing so we will come to acquire an even better understanding for why UFOs have become such an enduring part of our mythology and why they continue to hold such fascination for so many.

Understanding the Human Factor

By far, the most overwhelming evidence for the existence of extraterrestrials comes from eyewitness accounts, which many people consider to be not only valid scientific evidence but, when taken in their entirety, make the case for extraterrestrials seemingly ironclad. After all, millions of people around the world can't *all* be wrong about what they've seen, can they?

Well, theoretically at least, yes, they can. While eyewitness accounts by competent and trained observers need to be taken seriously, the fact is that such evidence does not constitute proof of extraterrestrial visitation, regardless of the quality of the observer.

Human beings have several serious flaws that make them frequently poor observers of aerial phenomena. Perhaps the most serious of these is their propensity toward possessing unshakable confidence in their own powers of observation. It is a frequently observed phenomenon that witnesses often remain adamant in their belief that what they saw was without question extraterrestrial in origin long after a plausible alternative explanation has been offered and, in some cases, even demonstrated. We are creatures of habit who dislike uncertainty in the things we encounter and so often chafe at the idea that we might be as easily fooled as the next person—especially if we consider ourselves to be a trained observer such as a pilot, police officer, or a scientist. As a result, while we are often quick to dismiss other people's experiences, we are often willing to fight to the death for the authenticity of our own experience. However, even the most astute person can be fooled by their own eyes, especially when encountering the unexpected, and regardless of how well "trained" an observer they consider themselves to be.

Second, people are natural storytellers with an innate tendency to embellish and exaggerate what they see. As such, an unexplained light that seems to be following one's car suddenly becomes a spacecraft of extraterrestrial origin, and the shimmer of sunlight bouncing off an aircraft fuselage grows with each retelling into a silver disk of unquestionably extraterrestrial origins. It's human nature to want to be entertaining as well as informative, which can have the unfortunate side effect of turning even the most mundane experience into an exciting story of an extraterrestrial encounter. This is not an effort to defraud—observers genuinely believe they are accurately describing what they saw—but a normal and, some might say, natural part of what it is to be human.

Finally, the human brain is a poor place for storing memories. Even after only a short interval of time, the most carefully noted details of any observed phenomena start to fade. Dates and times become confused, sequences of events jumbled, minor but significant details forgotten until, in the end, the story becomes a distant recollection lacking in clarity—especially in older people whose memories may already be starting to fail due to the natural entropy of aging. The event itself will likely stick in the memory but with the passage of time it becomes increasingly difficult to recall the incident with the degree of accuracy one was able to do in its immediate aftermath, and without fellow witnesses or some sort of hard evidence to rely upon, the details are inevitably going to be fuzzy or even forgotten.

Self-Deception

Then there is the psychological factor to take into account. There are those who possess such a deep desire to see "something" that they are capable of inducing a sort of self-delusion to feed their obsession—a phenomenon that is especially true of things that have taken on an almost legendary status in our culture such as UFOs. Therefore, just as people who report seeing Bigfoot, sea serpents, or ghosts often find the experience to be life-altering, so too, it is argued, may some people be driven by their fervent desire to be part of something mysterious and extraordinary that it makes them especially good candidates for suggestion and hysteria.

Of course, the fact that a witness may already be favorably inclined toward believing in UFOs does not, in and of itself, automatically render their experience unreliable, but it should be enough to give the seasoned investigator reason to approach with caution the testimony of even the best witnesses. When it comes to UFOs (or any extraordinary or paranormal claims, for that matter), we must be careful not to let our own predispositions get the best of us. Instead, we should listen carefully to what people tell us, look over the evidence as best we can, consider the credibility of the witness, and then decide what to accept as credible. There is nothing wrong with being overly cautious, especially with a subject as fraught with imagination and fear as the UFO field has become.

Additionally, we must take into account that there are people who possess what's commonly called a "fantasy-prone" personality. Such a person suffers a sort of deep-set and self-sustaining delusion that is constantly fed by their fascination with a particular subject and a willingness to believe absolutely everything told to them without hesitation, all designed to give their lives meaning and provide an anchor for their ego. Conspiracists tend toward this condition, which they are able to maintain by interpreting suppositions as fact and constructing ever more sophisticated and complex theories until, in the end, they largely lose the ability to differentiate reality from fantasy. As such, the possibility that one is dealing with a fantasy-prone personality needs to be factored into the equation, especially in those cases in which witnesses appear to be eccentric, highly excitable, or somewhat paranoid.

Yet this explanation goes only so far, for while there are fantasy-prone and highly excitable individuals who fit this description, anyone who has researched UFOs for any length of time will tell you that such individuals are the exception rather than the rule. Just as it is with people who encounter Bigfoot, sea serpents, and ghosts, most did not seek out nor anticipate the encounter, but simply found themselves having an experience they were not prepared for. Additionally, it doesn't explain those observations made by witnesses known for their levelheadedness and ability to remain calm under even the most stressful situations, making the self-delusion theory too simplistic an answer to cover every contingency, especially when there are multiple witnesses of impeccable credentials sharing similar experiences.

Hoaxing

It is a poorly kept secret that there are individuals who enjoy deceiving others. Some do it for the possibility of financial gain and the opportunity to acquire some fleeting fame, others to test their own cleverness and ability to deceive others, and finally, some do it just for the sheer fun of pulling off a great con. More often than not, however, hoaxing is done in an effort to prove a point (usually how foolish, stupid, or gullible others may be), which is a little game we humans frequently play on ourselves that often makes getting at the truth difficult, especially as the tools available for fooling each other grow increasingly sophisticated and affordable and the pure joy of besting others proves so enticing to a clever but tiny minority of people. As such, while pure hoaxes are uncommon, one must always be careful not to be duped whenever dealing with any extraordinary claim or when confronted with what appears, at first glance, to be hard evidence of some kind.

Of course, a good UFO investigator is aware of this and so is always on the lookout for any inconsistency or incongruities in a story, while photographic evidence is carefully scrutinized for any signs of tampering or foul play. Very few people are capable of keeping a running gag going for any length of time, and they almost always overlook some small detail that unravels the whole thing, making it extremely difficult to pull off a good hoax. That's not to say there haven't been some notable hoaxing successes, but if one approaches every story with a healthy degree of skepticism to begin with, the chances of a joke making it onto the evening news can usually be kept quite small.

Unfortunately, it appears that unique subject matter in general—such as the paranormal and UFOs—is a natural magnet for hoaxers (as well as the emotionally unstable), with ever more elaborate and sophisticated frauds being perpetrated upon an often all-too-eager-to-believe public. The author himself was once taken in by some seemingly very authentic footage of an alleged UFO disk supposedly shot over the country of Haiti in 2007, only to discover after a few days of digging that the footage was simply the result of some exceptional CGI work (much to my great regret). This taught me that accepting any story or piece of footage at face value is going to inevitably result in being victimized by a clever con man, as many a researcher—including myself—has learned the hard way.

Of course, what makes it even possible for hoaxers to enjoy such success is in large part due to another common human foible: our misplaced confidence in our ability to detect a tall tale when we hear one. While most of us consider ourselves too smart to be fooled, the sad fact is that, as a rule, most people are not particularly adept at consistently telling when they are having their leg pulled or recognizing when they are in the presence of a truly disturbed or fantasy-prone personality. Most naturally assume people are being honest with them—especially when such a person seems sincere or is perceived to be a credentialed "expert" in their field. Trust is a wonderful thing, but when it is misplaced or granted too easily, it can often result in all sorts of unfortunate consequences—as many who have been duped by an "expert eyewitness" have discovered to their great regret (and, sometimes, financial loss).

Most of the time, hoaxers are not the problem, however, but rather our own natural human propensity toward deceiving ourselves. It seems that human nature has built into its very essence an innate desire to *want* certain things to be true—or not be true— based upon our personal biases, beliefs, and predispositions. This is why the ardent believer will be so quick to embrace even the most outlandish story and why the hardcore skeptic will refuse to consider even the most credible report from a highly reliable witness out of hand; we have all adopted a world view that has been shaped by our upbringing, environment, experiences, and even our basic personality, which is what creates the unique prism we use to determine what we are willing to accept as true or reject as untrue.

The Problem with "Expert" Witnesses

Another weakness in the UFO phenomenon has been its dependence upon testimony given by "expert" witnesses, which is often considered to be far more valuable than the accounts given by the average person. As such, the words of an airline pilot or police officer are given far more weight than those of a truck driver or a repairman, even though there is no solid evidence that such people are necessarily better witnesses (or, by extension, that truck drivers and repairmen make less credible witnesses).

Undoubtedly, many people will disagree with such a statement because it appears, at least at first thought, to be counterintuitive. After all, wouldn't a trained pilot *naturally* be in a better position than a truck driver to determine the true nature of an aerial phenomenon?

While it is true that an experienced pilot would probably be less likely than most people to mistake another aircraft or other common aerial phenomenon for a UFO, there is no evidence that the pilot couldn't be just as mistaken about what he or she saw as would anyone else. After all, the abrupt appearance of an unexpected object is as unnatural to a pilot as it would be to a layperson, making a pilot as prone to exaggeration and wild guessing as any of the pilot's passengers. Even the best pilots get excited when encountering something unexpected, and gauging distances, size, and speed from the cockpit of an aircraft is no easy task, especially when done in haste. Rates of climb and airspeed can be wildly misjudged, especially in the darkness. Pilots are, after all, only human, and as such, even the most seasoned among them are capable of being fooled by common aerial phenomena, particularly in situations in which fear and uncertainty may be in play.

Police officers are also frequently afforded far greater leeway in making their claims than are civilian witnesses, and usually deservedly so. After all, police officers are specifically trained to be careful observers, so it is assumed that when they see something inexplicable they are going to be far more careful about what they describe—and, supposedly, less prone to exaggeration, guessing, and hysteria—than would be the average citizen. However, this is not necessarily true; like pilots, police officers are as capable of being frightened by something unexpected as anyone else. Cops are trained to observe people and unusual behavior, not inexplicable lights in the sky, so there is no compelling reason they couldn't be just as prone to exaggeration and wild guesses as a civilian would be, making their testimony no better—or worse, for that matter— than anyone else's.

And as far as military observers go, reliability is even less of a given. As a veteran myself, I know for a fact that military people are often no better observers of unusual phenomenon than anyone else. Considering that the average age of an enlisted man or woman in the armed forces today is around twenty and that most fighter pilots—the military personnel most likely to encounter a UFO directly—are usually under thirty years of age, they may, in fact, be even less reliable witnesses than their more mature civilian counterparts. That's not to imply that the testimony of a young person should be immediately suspect, but that it is always wise to take such factors as maturity and the natural tendency toward imagination and gullibility found in young people in general into account when gauging the credibility of any story.

Misidentification of Natural Phenomena

While hoaxes, imagination, mass delusion, and hysteria may account for some UFO reports, they are factors in only a tiny fraction of the many hundreds—and sometimes thousands—of UFO reports made worldwide each year. The fact is that most UFOs are usually the misidentification of some astronomical/natural phenomenon or man-made object or device of some kind.

While many dismiss such a statement as a simplistic attempt to skirt the issue or, worse, a carefully contrived and orchestrated effort at debunking the entire phenomenon, the fact is that many, if not most, UFOs can usually be explained away as unusually bright stars and planets, high-altitude balloons, orbiting satellites, and misidentified aircraft. As such, it's important we examine each of these possibilities in order, if only in an effort to better appreciate the difficulties investigators frequently face when looking at the phenomenon from a scientific perspective. This list is by no means exhaustive, but I believe it does account for the bulk of UFO sightings reported over the years.

The Planet Venus

It's no coincidence that UFO reports go up sharply whenever Venus makes an especially bright appearance in the night sky, so this explanation is not as far-fetched as it seems. Under the proper conditions, Venus can be among the brightest objects in the sky—especially on a moonless night—and has even been known to be visible in the daytime under the proper conditions, making it a frequent explanation for many a mysterious "bright light in the sky." For those already predisposed toward accepting any unusual light in the sky as a potential close encounter, Venus makes an especially good candidate for being a UFO—particularly when it is seen low on the horizon from a moving automobile (when it can appear to be following) or on a partly cloudy night when it will seem to abruptly appear and disappear as fast-moving clouds obscure it from view. Additionally, it can be extremely difficult to convince people that the bright light in the sky they saw "chasing them" was merely sunlight reflecting off a nearby planet, largely because of the natural human reluctance to admit error as well as the trauma such an experience can induce.

Unfortunately, this explanation has provided many in the skeptical community a convenient "catch-all" explanation for almost any mysterious light seen in the sky (especially when Venus is present). This, however, is a bit disingenuous: Venus is a fixed point of light and as such is unlikely to be mistaken as a UFO by those who possess some basic knowledge of astronomy, nor is it likely to be interpreted as anything other than what it is by pilots or other trained observers. Additionally, it is also a simple matter of determining Venus's location and luminosity on any given evening, making it a fairly easy task either to confirm or reject it as a possible explanation. As such, it is not generally a good explanation for the better eyewitness accounts reported—especially in those cases in which an unidentified light is seen to perform erratic or high-speed maneuvers.

Meteors, Comets, and Fireballs

This is a less common explanation, especially since most people are familiar with meteors (or "shooting stars" as they are commonly called) and so are unlikely to mistake one for a UFO. Comets[11] are even less likely to be mistaken for UFOs, especially since comets remain fixed in the sky, can be seen for weeks at a time, and are usually not particularly bright in the first place. A fireball, however— basically a large, brightly lit meteor observed at close range—is a better candidate, especially as a fireball can be very bright, last sev-

---

11.   It's been my experience that many people use the terms *meteor* and *comet* interchangeably. They are, of course, two entirely separate phenomena.

eral seconds, appear to split into smaller pieces, and even abruptly disappear from sight as though it were "zooming away at great speed," as many UFO witnesses describe. I'd imagine seeing a fire-ball head-on would be particularly impressive, as it would appear to be an extremely bright and slow-moving object that suddenly vanishes from view. Such astronomical phenomena are not, however, adequate explanations for an object that makes abrupt course changes in mid-flight, changes color (or shows multiple colors), or that lasts more than a few seconds, and as such constitute only a very tiny fraction of all UFO reports.

Lenticular Clouds

Technically known as *altocumulus standing lenticularis*, lenticular clouds are stationary lens-shaped clouds that form at high altitudes, normally where stable, moist air flows over a mountain or a range of mountains. Usually these air currents form long strings of clouds known as a *wave cloud*, but sometimes, under the right conditions of wind and thermal currents, they can take on a roundish or oval shape that can appear extraordinarily unnatural and even "saucer-like," which in turn can be confused for an extremely large disk by people unfamiliar with such meteorological phenomena. Further, their exotic nature is often enhanced when seen alone against a clear blue sky or when they quickly dissipate due to rapidly chang-ing air patterns, giving the impression that they have "sped away." Only those entirely unfamiliar with this phenomenon are likely to be fooled by a lenticular cloud, however, especially once they observe one for a while and realize it is neither moving nor appears to be mechanical in nature. Still, for the unaware, it can be a strange sight and one that might be easily confused for something otherworldly.

Ball Lightning

Among the more unusual and lesser understood electrical curi-osities known to science is something called "ball lightning," a phe-nomenon that has only been identified within the last fifty years or so. Basically, ball lightning is a sphere of static electricity that has the ability to glow intensely for several minutes at a time and, when seen in broad daylight, can even take on a fluid, silvery-like sheen that can be easily mistaken for metal, giving it a "disk-like" appearance. Additionally, though usually seen to move randomly, sometimes the discharge is described as being attracted to a certain object—normally an aircraft—and even matching it in terms of speed and maneuvers, thereby giving it the impression of being under intelligent control. Commonly described as spherical, ovoid, teardrop, or rod-like in shape, and with colors that vary from red to yellow (though other colors have been observed), it's not difficult to see how ball lightning could easily be mistaken for an unnatural object, especially after it disperses, is absorbed into something, or—though rarely—vanishes in an explosion. As such, ball lightning appears to be a perfectly adequate explanation for some of the more erratic lights seen in the sky—especially those observed from aircraft.

The only drawback to this explanation is that such displays are uncommon and, being that these balls of energy are usually no larger than a basketball (though some have been reported as large as ten meters in diameter), it makes it difficult to imagine they could be interpreted as alien spacecraft. In the darkness, however, judging size and distance can be difficult, making a relatively small object appear much larger and farther away than it actually is, so the prospect of mistaking a tiny ball of static electricity for a much larger UFO is not out of the question.

Weather Balloons

Although frequently lampooned as the most simplistic of explanations for UFOs, the fact is that helium-filled weather balloons make excellent UFOs, especially when seen from below when their spherical shapes can appear especially disk-like. Further, these balloons can be quite large, are often coated in a highly reflective material (giving them a polished or shiny appearance), and can fly at altitudes as high as 120,000 feet, where winds aloft can sometimes push them along at hundreds of knots, giving them the illusion of moving at high speeds. Further, when seen moving through a partly cloudy sky where winds can blow in different directions at different altitudes, sometimes pushing clouds in one direction and a balloon in the opposite, the illusion of high speed is even further enhanced. More than once, I have had to study a fast-moving object in the sky for some time before determining it to be something as innocuous as a balloon, so the weather-balloon theory is not only valid but needs to be taken seriously.

In fact, a weather balloon may have been responsible for one of the more famous—and tragic—UFO incidents on record. During the late 1940s, the U.S. military began experimenting with a particularly large balloon made of reflective aluminum and nearly one hundred feet in diameter called *Skyhook*, which may have been partially responsible for the death of twenty-five-year-old Kentucky Air National Guard pilot Captain Thomas F. Mantell near Franklin, Kentucky, on January 7, 1948. In this famous incident, Captain Mantell, flying a World War II–era piston-driven P-51 fighter, apparently spotted one of these balloons flying at high altitude and, mistaking it for a silver saucer (which is what the balloon would have looked like from his position well below), gave chase. In the course of closing in on the "UFO," he flew above the altitude acceptable to fly without oxygen, apparently blacked out, and the plane went into an unrecoverable dive, crashing into the ground at high speed and killing him instantly.

While some have disputed this explanation, noting that no particular Skyhook balloon could be conclusively identified as being in the area in question during Mantell's pursuit, investigators later determined the Skyhook solution to be the most plausible explanation: the balloons were consistent with his description of the object, and several such balloons were later shown to have been launched in nearby Ohio earlier that day. Since the Skyhook balloons were secret at the time, however, neither Mantell nor the other observers in the air-control tower would have been able to identify the UFO as a Skyhook balloon, making it appear that the young pilot had lost his life at the hands of extraterrestrials.

Of course, balloons are not always a good answer for a UFO. Certainly, they are not capable of making ninety-degree turns or of suddenly zooming out of sight (though they are frequently easy to lose sight of and may abruptly explode due to heating), nor do they normally glow in the dark, so the weather balloon explanation must be used sparingly. Still, considering their very "un-aircraft-like" characteristics and the novelty of seeing a large weather balloon silently hovering high in the atmosphere, balloons may account for far more sightings than some might suspect.

Satellites

As the demand for improved communications, weather forecasting, and aerial surveillance grows, the orbital lanes around our planet are growing increasingly cluttered with a wide array of fast-moving and highly reflective satellites of all sizes and configurations. To give you some idea of how cluttered our skies are getting, the United States Space Surveillance Network currently tracks more than *eight thousand* man-made objects orbiting the planet, of which about 7 percent (approximately 560) are operational satellites.

Often trapped in their orbits for years at a time, however, these silent sentinels of the skies can usually be picked out by anyone with a pair of binoculars and some patience, so they are not an uncommon sight. Additionally, as they can often appear to pulsate in intensity (a natural illusion created by atmospheric inversion layers) and even "wink out" when their angle to the sun changes, they can sometimes be mistaken for UFOs. Of course, this wouldn't explain those wandering lights that are seen to abruptly change direction (something satellites are incapable of doing), but they doubtlessly have accounted for a great many UFO sightings over the years.

Flares

Military aircraft often drop flares while conducting night training operations (or, in combat areas, as a means of diverting heat-seeking missiles). These flares, unlike the tiny ones used to mark highway obstacles or for emergency use, are quite large and will burn brightly for up to thirty minutes at a time and, when suspended from parachutes, can remain airborne for some time. As such, if dropped in a cluster, they can take on a beaded-necklace effect that gives them the impression of either aircraft hovering in formation or, if close enough together, can even appear to be a string of running lights or "portholes." To a public generally unfamiliar with such ordnance and its characteristics, however, the effect can be spectacular and even frightening, making flares an especially good candidate to be mistaken for a UFO. This, in fact, may be the explanation behind the mysterious lights that were seen hanging over Phoenix, Arizona, in 1997 (which does in fact lie near a military training ground where evening bombing exercises are frequently held).[12]

Swamp Gas

Perhaps the least successful explanation offered by science to explain away some sightings, swamp gas is essentially a collection of methane (characteristically, swamp gas is found in peat bogs, mud flats, marshes, and swamps—wherever stagnant water coincides with the decay of organic matter) that can, under certain conditions, take on a mildly luminous appearance and appear to hover just above the ground. However, this effect has never been seriously accepted by either proponents or opponents of the UFO phenomenon as a particularly plausible explanation, largely due to the small size, general rarity, and lack of movement of swamp gas. While such an unusual sight might be mistaken for a UFO by someone unfamiliar

---

12. Curiously, even when the Air Force admitted that they had dropped flares in the course of carrying out night training exercises in the area that evening, the explanation was largely rejected by a large segment of the UFO community as yet another government cover-up, demonstrating how cynical many ufologists have become in trusting their own military.

with the phenomenon, it appears unlikely to account for more than a tiny percentage of all sightings. Still, it is something to take into account, especially if one should spot something unusual over the Florida Everglades or a Louisiana bayou.

Birds, Lens Flare, Reflections, and Other Abnormalities

Few people can accept the possibility that something as seemingly commonplace as a bird could be mistaken for a UFO, but it must be realized that, under certain circumstances—and especially when flying at very high altitudes (some birds have been spotted flying as high as forty thousand feet or more)—birds can be highly reflective and, especially when wet, can even appear to glisten like metal, giving them an "artificial" or metallic appearance. Additionally, bits of tinfoil or panels of corrugated metal driven skyward by high winds and strong updrafts, falling chunks of ice broken off from a high-altitude airliner, and other bits of aerial flotsam can also take on a silvery sheen and appear quite luminescent, making them occasional candidates for flying disks. Even cockpit lights reflecting off a canopy have been misidentified as high-speed UFOs (especially in the early years of UFO pursuits), making it especially important that observers take their time before declaring any airborne object or light a UFO.

Aircraft

While it is difficult to imagine that anyone could mistake a modern airliner or military jet for an extraterrestrial vehicle, there are circumstances in which an aircraft can appear quite unusual, particularly to a highly excitable observer. For example, anyone who has ever seen a jet's landing lights diffused by thick fog (or suddenly turned off during a steep ascent, making the aircraft appear to abruptly vanish) could easily imagine they are witnessing something otherworldly. Additionally, an aircraft flying through thick clouds on a dark and windy night (when the sound of engines is often masked) could easily appear as a mysterious, bright object winking on and off and changing brightness as it moves silently through the darkness. In daytime also, identifying a mysterious object in the sky as an aircraft can also be problematic; when flying at high altitude (where engine noise is often indiscernible) on a bright and sunny day, the brushed aluminum fuselage and wings of an aircraft can give off an eerie sheen which, when combined with the fact that most aircraft's navigation lights are invisible in daytime, can make it appear to be a silvery object moving swiftly across the sky. Also, if seen straight on, an aircraft can appear to be hanging motionless, at least until it makes a sudden turn, thereby mimicking the sudden stops and start movement often associated with UFOs and further enhancing its otherworldly effect.

While fixed-wing aircraft are less likely to be misinterpreted as UFOs by an increasingly savvy flying public today, they were undoubtedly the cause of many early UFO reports when aircraft were less common and, as such, more "unusual." Further, blimps, helicopters, and VTOL[13] aircraft are also frequently mistaken as UFOs due to their unconventional flight characteristics—in particular their ability to hover and then suddenly fly away. Normally, one has only to watch these vehicles for a few minutes to ascertain their true identity, but the highly excitable may never spend those few minutes before deciding they are seeing an alien spacecraft. Additionally, it is likely that over the next few decades lighter-than-air technology will become increasingly evident as both unmanned/stationary and manned/commercial airships—some many times larger than modern airliners—begin to make their appearance in our skies. I'd imagine that until the public becomes aware of and comfortable with this reemerging technology, reports of airships being mistaken for UFOs will become increasingly common as well.

---

13. VTOL (Vertical Take-Off and Landing) aircraft combine elements of fixed-wing aircraft and helicopters, making them capable of both hovering and high-speed forward flight.

Experimental Military Aircraft

It's no secret that ever since the advent of flight over a century ago, the U.S. military has been hard at work developing and testing new and ever-improved versions of its aircraft, along with other "cutting-edge" technologies, all with an eye on keeping ahead of—or at least pace with—real or potential adversaries. Not surprisingly, this has led to a vast array of often unusual or, at the very least, unconventional designs being introduced, which no doubt has resulted in more than a few UFO reports over the years. This hypothesis was especially popular during the early years of ufology, when it was widely assumed—even by our own government—that the strange vehicles seen in the skies were either test flights of captured Nazi aircraft or new and exotic Soviet vehicles capable of penetrating our airspace with impunity. In fact, the Air Force's first official attempt to investigate UFOs—Project Sign—worked from the premise that UFOs were precisely such weapons, thus necessitating both the urgency and the secrecy under which Project Sign operated.

The hypothesis does have a few flaws, however. First, the flight characteristics of reported UFOs are so far beyond our present technological capabilities that it is quickly apparent they are not of terrestrial manufacture. Even the most modern fighter aircraft cannot make ninety-degree turns or ascend out of sight within mere seconds, making the "secret weapon" hypothesis increasingly problematic. Second, advanced aircraft are usually not extraordinarily alien in appearance. They may be unconventional looking—such as the Stealth fighter and the B-2 "flying wing" bomber—but for the most part advanced aircraft maintain a fairly traditional appearance, carry the same running and landing light configurations, and make much the same noises as do other aircraft. Truly exotic and unconventional designs (the saucer shape, for example) have consistently proven to be unstable configurations, aeronautically speaking, and were quickly abandoned. Third, most test flights—especially those of the highest levels of secrecy—are normally performed over sparsely populated areas of the country, making their appearance over large population centers unlikely. The military has always been careful to ensure its test flights receive as little attention as possible—for painfully obvious reasons—so it's a near certainty that the unusual craft you see doing right-angle turns, darting at incredible speeds across the sky, and changing color and intensity are not one of ours (or anyone else's, for that matter). While undoubtedly a few UFOs may well be misidentifications of secret aircraft on test flights, it's difficult to see how these would account for more than a tiny percentage of all reports.

Conclusions

The point to be made here is that it is not difficult to see how many well-intentioned and sincere people can be misled by even the most common of astronomical, meteorological, or aerial phenomena, as well as how even the best trained observers are frequently no better than the common layperson at identifying such objects, thereby bolstering the skeptics' case. However, it is also a fact that while hoaxes, delusion, and misidentification of natural or manmade objects do account for most UFO reports, they do not explain them all. There are those sightings that, despite the best efforts of science and the military to explain away, simply defy explanation and must be looked at more closely. Even the Air Force's own Project Blue Book couldn't find plausible explanations for some 6 percent of all sightings, and if the Air Force couldn't explain them—despite the many resources at their command (and, arguably, an innate desire to want to explain them away)—it would be a mistake for the skeptic to dismiss them out of hand by assuming the Air Force simply "missed something." That's neither fair nor honest, but merely an effort to avoid having to deal with the larger issue involved.

However, that's not the end of the debate nor the end of the debunking community's practical objections to the phenomena. The prospect of extraterrestrial visitation brings up other difficulties as well, each of which we will need to address before we can move on.

chapter six

Practical Objections to UFOs

One question often asked is, if extraterrestrials are in orbit around our planet observing us from space, why aren't they occasionally observed by astronomers? (Or, for that matter, why aren't they commonly detected on radar and spotted by reconnaissance satellites?) After all, if there are, as some suggest, many races watching over us at any given moment, our skies should be abuzz with their craft, making their ability to remain undetectable to us highly suspect—especially at our current level of technology. Additionally, if they have landed on our planet—as many ufologists maintain—why don't they leave trace elements of having done so in the form of landing-pad prints or scorched grass, as any mechanical device should do? In other words, if they're here, *why can't we find them?*

These are all reasonable questions that deserve honest answers. To answer them, however, will require us to look at the equation not just from our own limited perspective but from that of a technologically advanced extraterrestrial civilization. In effect, to understand how it might be possible for extraterrestrials to operate in our midst and yet effectively remain unseen, we need to "think like an alien."

The Sky-Gazer Dilemma

Some people imagine that there are literally thousands of men and women scanning the skies at any given moment, which should, at least in theory, make the prospect of any extraterrestrial device remaining unobserved extremely unlikely. Considering that there are nearly 250 observatories in the United States alone—along with thousands of telescopes being pointed skyward by an army of hobbyists and amateur astronomers on any given night—it stands to reason that at least a few unidentified and unusual lights should, from time to time, be spotted darting across the skies. However, astronomers rarely report observing anything strange during their studies of the night skies. It simply doesn't make sense that an alien craft could avoid detection with so many eyes focused on the heavens at any given moment.

This appears to be a reasonable objection until one more carefully considers the inherent nature of telescopes. Telescopes are specifically designed to observe objects at great distances—hundreds or even thousands of light years away—making them the ideal tool for investigating the universe. However, in being so far-sighted (hyperopic), they have extremely poor short-range vision, which makes them practically useless when the object in question may be relatively close. That's why things like aircraft, birds, insects, and even orbiting satellites can routinely pass in front of a telescope's lens and remain virtually invisible while a galaxy ten million light years away appears sharp and bright. Additionally, astronomers normally confine their observations to a particular planet or star, or concentrate on a single tiny sector of the heavens rather than on large expanses of sky when making their observations, giving them an extremely limited field of view. As such, anything that passes overhead is unlikely to make it into range, and even if it did, it would appear as little more than a brief blur of light as it quickly passed in and out of view. These facts alone are the main reason why even a thousand telescopes pointed heavenward are unlikely to pick up anything out of the ordinary; they simply aren't designed to, which is what makes them practically worthless as a tool for spotting UFOs.

Binoculars, however, are another matter. Unlike telescopes, binoculars are capable of bringing large quadrants of the sky into clear view, making them ideal for spotting objects like satellites and NEOs (Near-Earth Objects). Unfortunately, because of the large number of NEOs out there, simply spotting an unidentified point of light moving silently and swiftly through the night sky is not going to draw much attention from the vast majority of stargazers unless it does something unusual such as stop, abruptly change direction, change in intensity or color, or split into multiple points of light. As such, all an extraterrestrial craft would have to do to remain inconspicuous is simply maintain a steady, unwavering course through the sky—in effect, make itself look like just another high-altitude aircraft or an errant satellite.

Another point that many skeptics tend to overlook is the fact that they assume an extraterrestrial vehicle would or even *could* be seen in the night sky; in other words, they assume that an extraterrestrial craft would display running lights or be reflective in the same way known Earth objects are—an idea probably gleaned from movies and television programs, which tend to show alien spacecraft, usually for dramatic effect, both lit up like Christmas trees and garishly painted in highly reflective color schemes. A moment's consideration, however, should tell us how unlikely this would be: if extraterrestrials are truly intent on remaining unobserved, they would be foolhardy to display either exterior lighting or be coated in a reflective material. The greater likelihood is that an extraterrestrial craft would be coated with—or perhaps even built entirely out of—nonreflective material and display no exterior lighting of any kind. If it were to be spotted at all, most likely it would appear simply as a dark shape moving through the blackness of space with stars winking off and on again in sequence as it briefly passed in front of them, and could probably only be clearly seen if it happened to move in front of a significant light source such as the moon (and even then it would remain visible for only a few seconds).

Of course, stories of brightly lit UFOs are legion; in many cases, not only do they display extremely bright lights but sometimes multiple lights that change color. However, since it seems a fairly simple process to remain dark and inconspicuous, wouldn't this be indicative of a vehicle that *wants* to be seen rather than one that is simply transiting from point A to point B? After all, even a conventional aircraft can make itself practically invisible simply by turning off all exterior lighting, implying that any brightly lit UFO *fully intends to be seen* (for reasons that will become clearer later on).

While these explanations may work for nighttime observations, what about daytime appearances, when lighting would not be as major a factor and when nearly any object should be able to be easily spotted against a blue sky or as it passes in front of clouds? First, there are far fewer observers during the day than at night (meteorologists, forest-fire watchtower spotters, and air-traffic controllers being about the only daytime skygazers consistently out on a regular basis), greatly reducing the chances of someone spotting an unusual object passing overhead. Second, just as satellites remain invisible during the day, so would any vessel traveling in high Earth orbit remain similarly invisible from the ground, making the prospects of spotting a UFO unlikely unless it were flying extremely low. And, finally, it is reasonable to assume that any civilization that possessed the technology to transit the vast distances of space and perform the sorts of maneuvers commonly attributed to UFOs would undoubtedly possess the technology to mask their presence. This could be done either by adopting a form of camouflage that would render the UFOs virtually invisible to a ground observer (perhaps by being coated with a polymer that allows them to take on any color scheme instantaneously, much like a chameleon) or by bending light around themselves. As such, it remains reasonable to assume that a UFO is never going to be inadvertently seen, suggesting that those that are spotted either don't care if they are observed—which is doubtful—or they fully intend to be seen (which brings up a host of other questions that we will deal with later in the book).

The Radar Puzzle

One of the more perplexing dilemmas regarding UFOs over the years has been why they so rarely appear on radar, especially if they are flying low enough to be occasionally seen by ground observers and pilots. It's not unusual, for instance, for a craft to be seen by multiple witnesses, and yet local air-traffic control radars show nothing unusual, implying that either UFOs are impervious to radar or that the witnesses were simply mistaken in what they saw.

This phenomenon remained one of the most potent arguments against UFOs being physical machines until the introduction of stealth technology in the 1980s, at which point the mystery disappeared. Once it was demonstrated that flat surfaces tend to disperse radar waves in such a way as to effectively render an aircraft virtually invisible to radar, the stealthy nature of UFOs became more easily understandable. Of course, it's not known if a UFO reflects radar waves in the same way a stealth aircraft does or whether they are coated in a radar-absorbent material or perhaps even produce a force field that effectively absorbs the signal,[14] but the likelihood that they are as capable of rendering themselves invisible to radar—especially since we have this capability and must therefore assume this technology has been known to space-faring civilizations for centuries—must be considered not only plausible but almost a certainty.

The only question that remains, then, is not why UFOs don't normally appear on radar scopes, but *why they occasionally do*. Is this again something they allow, perhaps for our benefit, or could there be a more practical reason? For example, is it possible that due to

---

14. Since saucers are generally observed to be smooth and lack the flat surfaces and sharp angles of a stealth aircraft, this is probably the better assumption.

the nature of their propulsion system, maintaining "stealth mode" when in the vicinity of conventional aircraft might be harmful to that aircraft's electronic systems, at which point they choose to "go visible"? It's a well-established piece of UFO folklore that automobile engines frequently die in the presence of a UFO; could the same emissions that are responsible for rendering combustion engines inoperable be capable of doing the same to an aircraft in flight, thereby mandating a bit more caution be taken on the part of our visitors lest they inadvertently cause a mishap? It's an intriguing possibility.

In any case, if extraterrestrials are observing us, we should assume they can evade radar with the same ease with which they can remain invisible in both the day and night skies. There is simply no reason to imagine otherwise, especially if we are dealing with a technologically advanced civilization. In fact, it should be remarkable if they *lacked* these abilities—particularly stealth technology—considering that we, a far more primitive race, have perfected it.

Satellite Imaging

It has been frequently pointed out that were extraterrestrials truly flying overhead, one of our high-altitude reconnaissance satellites should periodically catch one on film as a UFO passes beneath it—a premise made all the more reasonable when we consider the capabilities of some of the newest satellites in our inventory (some reputedly capable of reading the license plate numbers off a moving car from sixty miles away).

Again, however, this fails to consider the question from the perspective of a technologically advanced race of extraterrestrials. If UFOs do have the ability to camouflage or otherwise make themselves "invisible" to ground observers, they should be able to do the same with equal ease with regard to satellites. If they have some sort of "chameleon-like" capabilities, for instance,[15] it's likely they have the ability to instantaneously assume a color scheme that would render them invisible from both above and below simultaneously, with different, constantly changing patterns appearing as they travel over differing landscapes at high speeds. Of course, if their ability to hide is a byproduct of simply bending light around themselves, the ability to remain unseen by a satellite is even less problematic.

However, a simpler reason UFOs would be unlikely to be caught by satellite imaging lies in the nature of satellites themselves; satellites are, by nature, confined to very precise and unchanging orbits that allow their whereabouts to be determined with split-second accuracy. In fact, it is precisely this predictability that makes it possible for our own military to keep hardware it does not want a potential enemy to see out of sight. One assumes that extraterrestrials would take advantage of this predictability as well, allowing them to fly around or above any active satellite with ease as they make their way around the planet.

The SETI Argument

For those not familiar with the term, SETI—an acronym for the Search for Extraterrestrial Intelligence—is the collective name for a number of organized efforts committed to detecting intelligent life through the use of radiotelescopes and deep-space receivers strategically located around the globe. In operation since the early 1960s, today the loosely coordinated effort is maintained around the clock by an international alliance of both professional and amateur astrologers and enthusiasts, all of them searching eagerly for any sort of transmission that could be definitively determined to be artificial in origin, thereby demonstrating the existence of at least one other advanced civilization in our galaxy.

---

15. Perhaps they are coated with a type of LCD material, making all surfaces effectively television screens!

As such, some skeptics maintain that if there truly are advanced civilizations out there, SETI scientists should have been able to pick up their signals by now. If Drake's equation is correct (see chapter 2) and there may be as many as *ten thousand* civilizations capable of communicating with us, it seems that the chances of picking up a signal from at least one of them should be excellent. The fact that forty years of careful listening has failed to produce as much as a whisper,[16] however, suggests to some that we are unique and, more significantly, alone in the universe.

This, however, is among the weakest argument against the prospect of intelligent life put forth by the skeptical community. First, it assumes that advanced civilizations use the same types of radio transmissions we do and would be broadcasting on a wavelength detectable to us. Such an assumption, however, is exactly that; they may operate on much higher or lower frequency ranges than we do, or use a system beyond our current means of receiving. Second, even if they did transmit in a frequency range we could receive, considering all the naturally occurring background noise produced by space, any signal, particularly if it is traveling many hundreds or even thousands of light years, may be too weak for us to detect with even our most powerful receivers. Presumably even the most powerful broadcasts have a limited range (after which any signal will simply be lost in the cacophony of normal background noise), so unless one of these advanced civilizations is within a few dozen light years from us—right next door in astronomical terms—and really "turned the volume up," so to speak, it's unlikely we would be able to hear them.

However, the main reason for the lack of success with SETI probably has more to do with timing than anything else. It's likely that even if another civilization did develop a communication system comparable to our own, at some point in its evolution it

---

16. Actually, a couple of brief, possibly artificial transmissions have been picked up over the years, but since they did not repeat themselves there was no means of confirming them as being of intelligent origin.

would replace such a primitive technology with a more efficient point-to-point laser or microwave system, making the window of time during which the older signals were broadcast—and, hence, perceivable to us—very brief. To better illustrate this dilemma, let's say a planet one hundred light years from us began beaming radio signals—either intentionally or inadvertently—into deep space a thousand years ago, and that it continued to do so for a full century and a half before replacing that technology with a more efficient and undetectable mode of communication. Since these signals would be traveling at the speed of light, they would have been detectable to us only between the ninth through tenth centuries, after which they would have ceased. Since this was long before we possessed the means to detect anything like a deep-space radio signal, the opportunity to hear their broadcasts is now lost to us, while our earliest signals to them will not reach their ears for another few decades yet. As such, in order for SETI to work, one needs to locate a civilization that is broadcasting within both the right frequency range and at precisely the right time or the entire effort is for naught—the point being that silence does not demonstrate a lack of alien intelligence but simply demonstrates just how difficult the quest to hear extraterrestrials actually is.

Of course, many scientists work from the premise that an extraterrestrial intelligence might use SETI to intentionally contact us, but this strikes me as even less plausible. If ETs have been observing us for several decades (and, by some accounts, much longer than that), they've had plenty of opportunity to send us a signal confirming their presence. The silence, then, suggests that they either don't exist or that they don't wish to contact us—at least not yet. However, it's important to continue to maintain SETI in case they one day change their mind or we get lucky and pick up a definitive signal from deep space. At a minimum, at least it lets them know we're listening, which I would imagine is considered a positive sign from their perspective.

Trace Elements Evidence

Skeptics are almost unanimous in their objections to UFOs in one area: the question of why, presuming these vehicles have occasionally set down upon the surface of the planet (and with some regularity, according to some), we don't find physical—or "trace"— evidence of that fact in the form of damaged or crushed plants, landing-pad footprints, or scorched earth. It might even be argued that, depending upon the nature of the power source used by a particular alien vessel, other clues in the form of radiation, electromagnetic anomalies in the surrounding environment, and even changes in the content or chemical composition of the soil itself might be expected, but to date there has been little or no such evidence forthcoming, implying once more that such "landings" are more likely figments of the imagination than literal events.

Of course, many ufologists maintain that such evidence *has* been collected at a handful of sites, but to date the samples that have been tested appear to be inconclusive or are largely dismissed by the scientific community as naturally occurring anomalies or suggestive of fraud (in other words, "planted" residue). Additionally, scientists correctly point out that soil can be altered for any number of natural reasons, and marks on the ground can be hoaxed or be the result of a more conventional vehicle setting down. In any case, it must be remembered that the burden of proof that an extraterrestrial object has interacted with the environment remains on the claimant, so until the UFO community can produce irrefutable evidence that a craft of some kind has left its mark on terra firma, I suspect that the scientific community will continue to maintain— and rightfully so—its skeptical position.

However, I do wonder if both sides aren't guilty of presumption with regard to such evidence. The fact of the matter is that we can't assume that a landed extraterrestrial craft would necessarily have *any* impact on the environment. First, without knowing the precise nature of its power source, it's impossible to say what sorts of effects a UFO's propulsion system might have on the underlying soil beneath it. For example, it's unlikely it would leave scorch marks, since such an effect is usually the result of combustion of some kind (like our own liquid and solid-fueled rockets, which would seem to be a conspicuously primitive form of propulsion for an advanced extraterrestrial race to use; in fact, I would think it most suspicious if scorch marks *were* found). But even if an alien craft left no discernible marks on the environment, shouldn't the landing site itself be "hot" with all sorts of energy anomalies or electromagnetic distortions of some kind?

Again, it all depends on what sort of propulsion system is used and how well-shielded the energy source is. Clearly an advanced technology should be able to mask any sort of electromagnetic signature or, at a minimum, it should dissipate very quickly after it leaves. As such, it would be very surprising if any anomalous electromagnetic readings were found at a landing site, especially hours or, as is the case in most landing cases, days after the alleged incident took place.

Then there is the question of radiation. Some people who claim to have come near a landed extraterrestrial craft have later reported to have suffered from radiation sickness and even of having acquired radiation burns, suggesting the presence of a nuclear-power source (which is something that should remain detectable for some time afterward). However, it is unlikely a nuclear-powered extraterrestrial craft would be "dirty" enough to put off enough radiation to harm a human. After all, we have been using nuclear power in submarines and other ships since the 1960s and have managed to not irradiate their crews, so we can assume any civilization advanced enough to get here would be able to adequately shield even the most powerful reactor. Of course, this is even assuming an extraterrestrial craft would use nuclear power as its chief source of energy in the first place. While it might be considered a reasonable power source from our perspective, most likely nuclear power would have been long ago superseded by other, cleaner, and more powerful energy sources that make use of anti-gravity or electromagnetism or some other exotic form of energy. Further, spacecraft are pelted by various types of radiation just by traveling through space: electromagnetic radiation produced by the sun, ultraviolet radiation, infrared radiation, gamma radiation, and even more exotic types such as cosmic radiation (or, as it is more commonly referred to, "cosmic rays"), some of which should seemingly be detectable in the environment afterward. However, regardless of what sorts of radiation an ET's spacecraft might pick up while in orbit, the descent through our atmosphere should dispel most of it in much the way a meteor (or the Space Shuttle) sheds any ambient radiation it might have acquired while in orbit. As such, since no one has ever suffered from radiation poisoning by handling a recently fallen meteorite or by touching the Space Shuttle after landing, one should not be similarly affected by inherent radiation from an alien ship.

However, as there are a few documented cases of people showing evidence of radiation poisoning as a result of a close encounter, doesn't that demonstrate they may have come in contact with an actual radioactive craft of some kind? I can't say with any degree of certainty, but could these effects be induced as part of the trauma of the experience? The mind/body link is a powerful one that can produce all kinds of genuine but idiomatic symptoms purely through the power of suggestion, so this needs to be considered. Additionally, it's important to note that while some people who have reported close encounters with alien hardware have reported being sickened or physically weakened by the experience, many others have not. Since there is no such thing as a radiation-resistant person, if UFOs emit radiation, then *everyone* coming in contact with them will be similarly affected—not just some. As such, those who claim to have been physically sickened by a UFO are more likely victims of their own imagination than they are of an exotic alien energy source.

Finally, even if an alien craft left no measurable effects on the environment, shouldn't it still leave landing-pad marks of some kind—footprints in the dirt, so to speak—indicative of a heavy machine having set down? Of course, such marks are occasionally reported, though most often they are not, further compounding the mystery and providing the skeptic with ready ammunition. However, this common objection is also a non-starter: first, we don't know if an extraterrestrial vehicle would even *have* landing pads or any sort of an undercarriage at all. It is because most of the landers we have sent to Mars and the moon in the past have all had retractable landing pads that we naturally assume a UFO would also have a similar type of tripod undercarriage, but this is pure speculation. Besides, even if they did have landing pads that left marks in the soil, wind and rain—along with inadvertent human contamination of a landing sight—would likely all combine to quickly erase all such marks from the area, making this objection even less problematic. However, a better guess, in my opinion, is that to avoid potentially damaging their craft and/or affecting the surface beneath it (thereby giving away their presence), an extraterrestrial vessel would never physically touch the ground at all, but simply hover on a cushion of air or rest upon some sort of electromagnetic force field. It could even employ a series of inflatable spheres to sit upon or even simply rest flat on its belly without the benefit of any sort of undercarriage at all, in which case identifiable imprints might be difficult to see (though one would imagine there should be some trampling of the flora at a landing site.) Purely speculative, I know, but not unreasonable.

Conclusions

What are we to make of all this? Clearly, the odds favor the proposition that life on some level does exist in the universe and, further, that the possibility of advanced life existing among the billions of star systems in just our galaxy alone is also extremely good. And if such a civilization (or, more likely, several) did exist, it is presumptuous to imagine it couldn't overcome not only the massive technological hurdles interstellar flight would pose but also manage to remain undetectable to us while it continued to study us from space.

As such, if extraterrestrials exist at all and they want to observe us while remaining unseen, they can do so with impunity. To suppose otherwise is to badly underestimate the technological capability of an alien race that may be potentially hundreds or even thousands of years ahead of us.

But that doesn't mean we've solved the UFO mystery. Just because the case can be made for extraterrestrial visitation, that doesn't mean it's an ongoing reality. There are a number of things that prevent us from making such a determination, the most conspicuous being how even the most advanced race of ETs could remain undetectable to the militaries of the world for nearly sixty years—especially considering the literally hundreds of thousands of reports filed over the decades. Surely some country's military would encounter something unusual at some point.

In fact, if some ufologists are to be believed, governments around the world—and specifically that of the United States—have known about extraterrestrials for decades but have chosen to keep such information suppressed for matters of public safety or national security. As such, it's time to look at the next piece of the UFO puzzle—conspiracy theories—to see how well they hold up under the light of logic.

PART TWO

Examining Government Conspiracies

If extraterrestrials are studying us, landing on our soil, being chased by our fighters, and possibly even abducting people, they're eventually going to make mistakes and so come into our awareness, and when they do it seems extremely unlikely that the military or even the science community itself wouldn't know something about it. However, if our government did have knowledge about—or even solid evidence of—an alien presence, would they tell us about it or choose to keep it quiet for any number of reasons? Or, for that matter, might they not even—as many contend—set about to purposely debunk the entire issue through a carefully orchestrated and well-coordinated disinformation program?

Since the issue of government cover-ups has become such a major element of the modern UFO movement over the last few years, it is important that we examine the issue in some detail to see if there is any validity to such beliefs. As such, in the next few chapters we will examine not only what the government *might* know about UFOs, but also consider the evidence and arguments for and against the possibility that extraterrestrials might even be working *with* our own government for some reason. We will also examine the prospect that UFOs may not only have crashed and been recovered by our military—and the technology in them studied and integrated into our own via reverse engineering—but even consider the allegations made by some that our government may be keeping dead aliens "on ice" and what that would mean were it true.

Since I'm not a government employee and lack access to classified documents, all I—or most writers on the subject, for that matter—can do is offer a few opinions, which many of my readers—especially those predisposed toward believing in conspiracies and distrustful of their government in general—may find untenable and even laughable. I offer them in any case, however, if only as another perspective on what has proven to be an emotional and often heated debate, in the hope that the reader will come away from the discussion with a clearer understanding of the enormity and complexity inherent to these issues and why it's important we consider them carefully before jumping to any conclusions.

chapter seven

Just How Much *Does* the Government Know?

To suggest that extraterrestrials could be orbiting our planet and even penetrating our airspace with impunity without being noticed by our own military—as well as those of a hundred other nations—would seem to strain credulity. Clearly, if these vehicles exist, our government knows about them or, at the very least, is aware of their existence even if they have no clear idea of what they are. Sixty years of sightings—including encounters that involved military aircraft and installations—makes this a virtual certainty.

However, the question of precisely how much is known remains a source for heated debate within the UFO community. Some maintain that government knowledge is fairly limited, but most take the position that the existence of extraterrestrials is not only known to our government but that there is a concerted effort to suppress that information on many levels—a position that is so pervasive within ufology that no book that pretends to be a thorough examination of the issue could be complete without taking a serious look at the possibility.

So, what is the *real* story? Has the government been in on it from the beginning, meticulously hiding what they know behind a façade of denial and misinformation, or are they only marginally interested in the phenomena, as they maintain? Of even greater importance, does our government possess alien artifacts they are even now in the process of carefully analyzing and incorporating into our own technologies, or is that all the product of tabloid journalism and overactive imaginations?

Before we proceed any further, it might be helpful to first examine the "official" history of the government's involvement in UFOs, if only to build a better foundation from which to pursue our investigation. While what follows is admittedly only the most bare-bones review, it should be enough to give the reader a basic picture of how much the government has been publicly involved with UFOs over the years—at least officially.

Projects Sign and Grudge:
The Beginning of Official Government Interest

Kenneth Arnold's "flying disks" did more than merely come to the attention of the American public in 1947; they also became a source of considerable interest to the military, which had a vested interest in determining how real they were and whether they posed a legitimate threat to national security. As such, within months of Arnold's encounter, the government began looking into the subject of UFOs or "flying disks"—as UFOs were frequently referred to in the early days—in earnest, not because they believed we were being invaded by Martians, but because of the possibility that they may have been Soviet devices of some kind. Considering that these vehicles seemed capable of penetrating American airspace with impunity and that we were in the midst of a very dangerous Cold War with Stalinist Russia, it's easy to see why an official study of the phenomenon would have made sense and was pursued with such speed and vigor—as well as secrecy.

Of course, since flying disks were airborne phenomena, the responsibility for investigating them naturally fell upon the newly formed United States Air Force, which undertook the job of formally examining UFO reports in January 1948 under the auspices of a program code-named Project Sign. While it is common today for many ufologists to dismiss all government investigations into UFOs as nothing more than efforts at debunking the entire issue, it appears that Project Sign was a genuine attempt to investigate "flying disks" in a thoroughly scientific manner, using some of the finest minds in the military and science to do just that. In fact, one of its earliest consultants was Ohio State University astronomer J. Allen Hynek, who, even though he had started his work as one of the idea's most ardent skeptics, was one day to become one of the more respected proponents of UFOs being of extraterrestrial origin.

In any case, Project Sign was to conduct investigations of hundreds of sightings over the next twelve months before the men associated with the program came to the conclusion—though not without considerable disagreement[17]—that UFOs, at least those that couldn't be explained away as hoaxes, naturally occurring weather phenomena, and man-made artifacts such as weather balloons or test planes, were probably not of Soviet manufacture and, as such, did not constitute a threat to the United States. Apparently satisfied that the phenomenon was solved—or, at a minimum, unimportant—and quickly growing tired of the whole issue of "flying saucers" in general, the Air Force cancelled Sign at the end of 1948, making it appear that official government interest in the whole affair was over.

However, things are never as simple as that when the government is involved. Due to growing public demand for some kind of

---

17. Curiously, although officially Project Sign came to no conclusion about UFOs (their final report stating that the existence of "flying saucers" could neither be confirmed nor denied), prior to that Sign officially claimed that UFOs were likely of extraterrestrial origin, and most of the project's personnel came to favor the extraterrestrial hypothesis before this opinion was rejected and Project Sign was dissolved.

answer as to what—if not Soviet weapons—flying disks were, the Air Force was forced to reconsider and a second program quickly followed in the wake of the now defunct Project Sign. In contrast to the earlier effort, however, and now more concerned with the prospect of panic if the public became convinced that UFOs were of alien origin, the Air Force decided to shift its approach from one of honest inquiry to outright skepticism and, in 1949, with the establishment of the perhaps more aptly named *Project Grudge*, the U.S. Air Force officially went into the debunking business—a role that some maintain it has yet to relinquish.

Some ufologists suggest Grudge was created in response to the Roswell—and possibly other—UFO crashes and recoveries made throughout the late 1940s, as part of a carefully orchestrated plan by the government to cover up what it had learned about these UFO "crash sites," but there is no real evidence for this. According to most historians, it instead appears that the military began to perceive "flying saucers" as more of a public-relations nuisance than anything else and worked according to that premise, even to the point of giving the assignment of investigating reports to largely disinterested officers anxious to finish their tour of duty and move on to more lucrative positions. Project Grudge, then, was probably less a covert government attempt to suppress the truth than a byproduct of indifference and outright annoyance with the whole affair.

By 1952, however, partially as a result of several spectacular and widely observed light formations being seen flying over Washington, D.C., and a general dissatisfaction with Grudge's negative thrust, the Air Force decided once more to change gears. Determined to investigate the phenomenon with a more even-handed approach and under the command of more sympathetic officers, Project Grudge was replaced by Project Blue Book, and the government was in the UFO business to stay—at least for a while.

Project Blue Book and the Condon Report

While many dismiss Project Blue Book as yet another feeble attempt by the military to cover up what it "really" knew about UFOs, it was actually a genuine—if undermanned—effort by the Air Force to investigate the many hundreds of reports received each year from both the public and the military, which it dutifully did for the next seventeen years. Though it never left its primary role of looking for natural explanations for each sighting (and while some of their explanations strained credulity at times), it was at least an attempt at objectivity, as evidenced by the fact that out of over twelve thousand reports logged by the time the program was terminated in 1969, Blue Book listed over seven hundred reports as still unexplained. While that's just 6 percent of the total, the fact that the Air Force was willing to admit to such a large number of unexplained sightings at least demonstrated that it wasn't simply dismissing UFOs out of hand.

By 1966, however—with the conflict in Southeast Asia growing more ominous each day—the military had more on its mind than extraterrestrials. After having investigated UFOs for twenty years and still uncertain what to make of them, the Air Force wanted out of the flying-saucer game for good. However, realizing that simply terminating the program would create more problems than it would solve, it decided to sponsor a civilian-run, scientific study designed to determine whether UFOs were of possible extraterrestrial origin, whether they constituted a threat to the United States, and whether they warranted further study. Officially titled the *Scientific Study of Unidentified Flying Objects* but more commonly known as the "Condon Report" (after the head of the study panel, University of Colorado physicist Edward Condon), the report, issued in 1968 after two years of study, proved to be the "out" the Air Force was looking for. Officially concluding that no UFO reports were anomalous and that further study of the subject would not be worthwhile—a conclusion enthusiastically endorsed by both the National Academy of Sciences and the scientific community in general—the report not only ended most "official" interest in UFOs, but it also gave the government the excuse it needed to cancel Project Blue Book, thereby ending its official role in the affair.

Ufologists cried foul, of course, claiming that the entire study was biased, unscientific, and shaped by the Air Force's expectations. Furthermore, critics have noted that Condon's summaries of UFO case studies were often sharply at odds with the reports they attempted to describe, making the whole effort appear to be little more than a government-funded attempt to discredit the entire phenomenon. Considering that it was no secret the military wanted to terminate Blue Book and that the Condon Committee, being funded by the Air Force (and largely staffed by scientists not favorably inclined toward the prospect of UFOs being of extraterrestrial origin), was prone toward dismissing the evidence in any case, the possibility that there was considerable pressure to come to the "proper" conclusions cannot be discounted.

However, the later claim made by some in the UFO community that the government never stopped investigating UFOs but used the Condon Report as a means of moving it underground—suggesting that it had found more to the story than it was publicly willing to admit—is unsubstantiated. Though it is likely the military continues to investigate certain incidents—especially those involving their own aircraft or that occur near sensitive military facilities—there is no indisputable evidence that the government or the military has maintained more than a cursory role in investigating the phenomenon after 1969. We will discuss this point in more detail later, but for now it is enough to understand that, at least as far as recorded history is concerned, the government's role in investigating UFOs ended in 1969 and that has remained the case ever since.

Civilian Investigative Efforts since Blue Book

With the government's official exit from the UFO game, the onus for investigating the phenomenon fell almost entirely upon the civilian community. Private civilian organizations like NICAP (National Investigations Committee on Aerial Phenomena) and APRO (Aerial Phenomena Research Organization) had been studying the phenomena since the 1950s, but both lacked either the resources or the manpower to do much more than collect reports and file them away for later study. With the end of Blue Book, however, and public interest in the subject burgeoning throughout the 1960s and 1970s (encouraged, perhaps, by such extraterrestrial-friendly movies as *Close Encounters of the Third Kind* and *Star Wars* and Gene Roddenberry's classic *Star Trek* franchise), a new crop of UFO organizations—many often no more than small clubs and loosely organized gatherings of enthusiasts—sprang up in America and around the world. Perhaps the largest of these is MUFON (Midwest UFO Network) out of Bellvue, Colorado, which, along with CUFOS (the J. Allen Hynek Center for UFO Studies) and FOFOR (the Fund for UFO Research), is part of the UFO Research Coalition—a collaborative effort by the three main UFO investigative organizations in the U.S. to share personnel and other research resources and to fund and promote the scientific study of the UFO phenomenon.

So what is the verdict on these efforts? While some useful research has been and continues to be accomplished, since so much of the UFO community is made up of hobbyists whose enthusiasm often exceeds their objectivity, results are, at best, mixed. Perhaps the biggest problem they face is one of credibility; whereas the Air Force was considered too quick to explain away UFOs—often without putting much thought into their explanations—it can be argued that many of the civilian organizations have gone too far the other way by showing a propensity to accept even the most outlandish claims with little or no substantiating evidence. This has had the unfortunate effect of leaving many ufologists open to charges of being highly gullible and even dishonest in their approach and methodologies. A second problem is that since many of the individuals who head these organizations have a very specific agenda in mind—that being to prove that extraterrestrials exist—the result is a marked lacked of objectivity when it comes to examining the evidence, further pushing the phenomenon from the realm of serious scientific consideration and doing great damage to the validity of the entire effort in the process.

Of course, the leadership within the UFO community has always been favorably inclined toward embracing the extraterrestrial position, but in the past that leadership was usually careful to present a balanced approach on the subject. For example, one of the early leaders within the UFO phenomenon, astronomer J. Allen Hynek, was applauded by even his most ardent skeptics for his careful approach and insistence that rigorous scientific investigative methods be employed in all cases, bringing a degree of legitimacy to the field that has apparently eroded considerably since his death in 1986. Since then, it appears the mantle has fallen to individuals who possess an almost quasi-religious fervor when it comes to authenticating the extraterrestrial hypothesis. This frequent lack of skepticism, combined with the fact that the UFO phenomenon has morphed into a multibillion dollar business and, in some cases, a type of New Age religion complete with its own sacred texts, self-declared gurus, and even holy sites (Roswell, New Mexico and Rachel, Nevada—home of Area 51—to name a few), has only resulted in a widening of the credibility gap between ufology and the scientific community. This has not only done considerable damage to the "cause" in some quarters, but it has made it increasingly difficult for the more moderate voices within the UFO community to be heard, much to the detriment of the entire phenomenon.

However, an even bigger problem has been a slow but steady shift within some of these organizations from being merely investigative bodies to becoming conspiracy groups. Ever since the Roswell "crash" story was reintroduced in 1980 (an incident we will examine in more detail later), the tendency within the UFO community has been to embrace the belief that the military has recovered crashed disks and even biological entities hidden away in various secret facilities around the country, and is currently "reverse engineering" the captured technology and integrating it into our modern inventions. Some have even gone to extremes and insist that the government is in league with extraterrestrials in keeping the public in the dark as to their activities and intentions, breeding an atmosphere of suspicion and paranoia that permits various government conspiracy theories to thrive.

The Majestic Documents

Perhaps no incident better illustrates this philosophy than does the "discovery" of a number of supposedly top-secret government documents known collectively as the Majestic 12 documents. Purported to be a series of secret correspondence between the White House and a select group of senior military officers and scientists during the 1940s and 1950s, in their entirety they are—if authentic—evidence that the government not only was aware of extraterrestrials as far back as 1947, but has been using the powers of the presidency to cover up that fact ever since. Even more, these letters imply that the military has recovered alien hardware in its possession and is intent on suppressing the information via a "disinformation" campaign designed to mislead the public as to the true extent of the government's involvement—a revelation that would obviously have profound political and scientific repercussions if true.

Problems with the documents soon emerged, however, and many have been subsequently exposed as hoaxes (though that remains hotly debated even among ufologists today), but their impact on the UFO community cannot be minimized. In fact, it's fair to say that these papers have done more to create an atmosphere of paranoia within ufology than any other aspect of the phenomenon. Of course, that doesn't discount the possibility that some of these documents might not be genuine, but it does force both proponents and opponents of the authenticity of the Majestic documents to take a deep look at themselves in an effort to determine how much they are letting often unsubstantiated accounts dictate their beliefs rather than simply looking at the evidence at hand in a balanced and objective manner. While it's outside the venue of this work to examine these documents in any detail, it is enough to note that while there is a good possibility that the government may indeed know more about UFOs than they're willing to admit, such can never be determined by appealing to what can only be considered the most suspicious of documentation, often acquired through largely unconventional means by people who not only have an agenda to pursue but credentials at risk should they be proven fraudulent. That alone should give anyone cause to be cautious where "secret government documents" are concerned.

In any case, I personally find it difficult to imagine that any government would be incompetent enough to leave such a paper trail in its wake—especially with something as shattering as extraworldly contact—or that it wouldn't have destroyed such documents long ago, but that is beside the point. What's important about the Majestic documents is the UFO community's willingness to so readily embrace them as fact and what that portends for the future. In framing the debate in such a way that one must either accept the most outrageous contentions of a wide-ranging government cover-up or reject extraterrestrials in toto largely eliminates any chance for real dialogue and only serves to widen the gap between believers and nonbelievers.

Of course, while not all ufologists accept the Majestic documents as legitimate or agree with the basic philosophy behind them, the voices of reason among such ufologists are being increasingly drowned out by the voices of those who see conspiracy everywhere, which has had the unfortunate effect of further driving away many potentially sympathetic listeners. We will examine a few of the most outlandish claims made by some of these groups in more detail later, but for now it is enough to recognize that once UFOs left the realm of objectivity and became fronts for a small but vocal group of conspiracy theorists, science and the UFO community essentially parted company, and it remains to be seen whether the two sides will ever be reconciled.

Regardless of what one believes about the authenticity of the Majestic documents or the largely anecdotal "evidence" in support of a massive government cover-up, however, that doesn't answer the question of just how involved the U.S.—and, presumably, foreign—governments are in the UFO phenomenon. Obviously, there is no way of knowing with any degree of certainty, but it might be helpful to examine just how the government deals with secrets, for in understanding how it deals with those things it doesn't want us to know about, we might be able to get a better idea of how difficult the process of keeping anything hidden for any length of time really is. While I have worked for the government and handled government documents while serving in the United States Navy, I am under no illusion that I possess anywhere near as complete an understanding of how the government classification works as some of my readers may. However, I have held top-secret clearances twice in my life which, along with being a careful observer, will hopefully give at least a few of my opinions some validity.

How the Government Keeps Its Secrets

It has been my experience that most people imagine that there are vast libraries of important "stuff" jammed into file cabinets that, if it became public knowledge, would blow the lid off everything from the JFK assassination to the precise whereabouts of Elvis. However, that was never my experience. While working with sensitive materials during my tenure in the Navy, what struck me most about dealing with confidential material was how routine most of it is: logistics reports, information requests, operational status—stuff like that. Very little of it, at least as far as I could tell, appeared likely to be of particular use to an adversary, yet all of it received the same classification rating as a matter of course regardless of how significant or routine the information was. In other words, everything was classified whether it discussed something as innocuous as how much fuel a particular ship took on during refueling operations or as important as an engineering breakdown onboard one of our attack submarines.

I soon came to understand the rationale behind this, however. First, it's a matter of convenience; it is far simpler to give every communication relating to a particular operation the same classification than it is to have people spend literally hours going through each communiqué and determining which classification level to give it (an important point considering the many thousands of messages a single day's operation can generate). But even more importantly, since it's not always clear what information might be useful to a potential adversary—even routine radio traffic, for example, can be of use when it is combined with other sources of information in painting an overall picture of fleet readiness, operational status, and capabilities—it is safer to just treat *everything* as if it were vital information rather than risk giving potentially sensitive information too low a classification and so allow even the smallest bit of potentially sensitive material to get into a potential adversary's hands.

I point this out merely as a means of correcting the general public's often distorted understanding of how the classification process works and why so much information that may currently be classified is unlikely to be of much value to UFO researchers. The sad fact is that most of what's tucked away in countless manila folders in warehouses around the country is mostly obsolete information that might have been important in 1956 but has since lost its urgency, or reams of routine reports that read as dry as the tax code. Obviously, anything as earth-shattering as crashed disks and recovered alien bodies is going to be buried so deep in the labyrinth of government security as to be for all practical purposes non-existent. As such, no matter how much investigators try to invoke the Freedom of Information Act in an effort to pry government secrets out of some bureaucrat's clutches, it is unlikely any of them are ever going to produce a document talking about, for example, the layout of the instrument panel on the recovered Rigelian saucer the Air Force has secreted away at Area 51.

Before proceeding further, however, it might be helpful to take a look at the official government classification system and the criteria behind each rating, if only to get a better understanding of what often proves to many people to be such a confusing and secretive process. Actually, it's really not at all that mysterious and is—for the most part—pretty straightforward. Although classification systems vary from country to country, most have levels corresponding to the following definitions:

Top Secret (TS)

The highest level of classification of material. Such material would cause "exceptionally grave damage" to national security if it were made publicly available. This would include information like precise invasion plans, exact capabilities of major weapons systems, names of undercover operatives; in other words, things that could really hurt the United States if the information were to be acquired by an unfriendly foreign power.

Secret

Such material would cause "serious damage" to national security if publicly available. This usually applies to material like specific battle tactics, forward-unit capability and disposition, modifications to major weapons systems, general information-gathering techniques, and such. Such information could cause real trouble if it were to be leaked, though not to the degree top-secret information would.

Confidential

This is material that would cause "damage" or be "prejudicial" to national security if publicly available. These are smaller matters like ship and troop movements, repair requests, general tactics, and a whole host of anything the government doesn't want one talking about to strangers. While most such information is largely trivial, it could still give an enemy some advantages they could use against us now or in the future.

Restricted
Material that would cause "undesirable effects" if publicly available. This level is similar to Confidential and is no longer used by the United States, which dropped it after World War II.

Unclassified
Not actually a classification level, it is used for government documents that can be viewed by anyone without a security clearance.

————

There are some who maintain that there are even higher levels of clearance than Top Secret, such as Above Top Secret and Eyes Only, but these are more the stuff of espionage novels than reality. The fact is that, according to Executive Order 13292,[18] there are no higher levels of classification. Additionally, depending on the level of classification, there are different rules controlling the level of clearance needed to view such information and how it must be stored, transmitted, and destroyed. Further, access is restricted on a "need to know" basis. In other words, simply possessing a clearance does not automatically authorize a person to view all material classified at or below that level unless they can demonstrate a legitimate "need to know" in addition to having the proper level of clearance. Also, there are sometimes additional constraints placed on access, such as Special Intelligence (SI), which protects intelligence sources and methods; No Foreign Disclosure (NOFORN), which protects diplomatically sensitive matters; and Originator Controlled Dissemination (ORCON), which ensures that the originator can track possessors of the information. There are a few other constraints used as well, mostly having to do with documents

---

18. Issued in 2003 by President George W. Bush, Executive Order 13292 recognizes only three levels of classification: Top Secret, Secret, and Confidential.

containing information about nuclear weapons (ESI or SIOP) and documents to be shared among NATO countries.

What drives researchers nuts, however, is in trying to understand the need for all the secrecy, especially for documents that may be decades old. After all, the argument goes, if the government doesn't have anything to hide, why is it so reluctant to provide unaltered documents or declassify ancient programs? Obviously, they must be hiding something—or so one might argue.

The truth is far less sinister. First, the sheer volume of documents involved—many millions by some accounts—makes the process of declassification extremely difficult and time-consuming. This is frequently why sixty-year-old projects are often still classified Top Secret long after the technology described in them is obsolete or their purpose is no longer relevant: there simply is no easy or quick process in place to declassify them, nor is there much incentive for doing so. Declassifying anything usually requires a panel to examine the documents in question (a lengthy process in cases in which documents may contain several thousand pages of information), delete any information still deemed even *potentially* sensitive, and then ensure that no other agency has some reason to keep the information classified. Since time is money and the government, one hopes, has more important things to do than read through reams of papers, you can see why the declassification process moves at a glacial pace. This is the main reason Project Mogul[19] wasn't declassified until 1994; the government simply had no incentive to do so until the whole Roswell thing got out of hand, forcing the Air Force to declassify Mogul in an apparently unsuccessful effort at making the whole affair "go away."

Another difficulty involved in trying to glean useful information from government vaults is the fact that not all government

---

19. Project Mogul, the Air Force's "official" explanation for the debris recovered at Roswell in 1947, was a top secret Air Force program designed to detect evidence of Soviet nuclear testing through the use of radar reflectors sent aloft by high-altitude weather balloons.

documents are retained. Many documents are destroyed as a matter of course for one very practical reason: were the government to keep every classified document it generated, it would create a mountain of paper tall enough to impede satellites in orbit. By way of example, while I was stationed onboard the Sixth Fleet flagship USS *Albany* in the late 1970s, scores of paper bags jammed full of radio traffic were routinely burned at sea each day, and for good reason: it was the quickest and most secure way to deal with the sheer volume of paper involved. Space onboard a warship is at a premium; I can only imagine the logistical nightmare it would have been to have kept every incoming message—which sometimes numbered in the hundreds each day—if we hadn't the means of burning classified materials at sea.

Of course, even though most government secrets are kept from the public because of the ponderous bureaucratic process required to declassify them, there are some documents the government *is* intent on consciously suppressing, but their rationale for doing so is not as sinister as many imagine. Usually this is information of a highly sensitive nature that could potentially compromise national security if leaked or documents that provide the names of intelligence operatives and other protected citizens that could mean their lives if they were publicly revealed. While it is likely that some of it might also be withheld for political reasons—especially if careers or credentials may be compromised by the information contained within them—for the most part the government suppresses information for what it considers to be the greater public good.[20]

Unfortunately, in most people's minds, this lack of openness is often perceived as deceit, with all the dark ramifications the term entails. This often results in the perception that not only is the

---

20. This gets into a tricky area, however, especially where civil libertarians are concerned. There are those who believe the government should be completely transparent as a means of maintaining accountability, and so they refuse to consider *any* classified material off-limits. This is an unrealistic and even potentially dangerous perspective, however, especially where issues of national security are concerned.

government an impediment toward learning the truth but also a malevolent force intent on ruthlessly suppressing that truth, thereby deepening the distrust between the public and its own government. It's no wonder, then, that repeated government denials of extraterrestrials, or "official" reports of and explanations for events (e.g., the Warren Report, the 9/11 Commission, Project Mogul, etc.), are routinely dismissed by large segments of the public as mere cover-ups. It really is a case of the government still paying for the sins of the past, both real and imagined.

Current Possibilities

While there's no way to know with any certainty what the government really does know about UFOs or to what extent they remain interested in them, it is likely the issue didn't just go away with the cancellation of Project Blue Book in 1969. Undoubtedly, the military has had encounters with UFOs since then and probably still maintains some interest in them, but to what degree is purely speculative.

While it seems unlikely the military would engage in the level of wholesale deceit implied by the Majestic documents, it's almost a certainty that they would have an interest in any encounter that involved one of their own aircraft, particularly if it took place near a sensitive military installation or if it involved any sort of pursuit; as such, I wouldn't be a bit surprised if it didn't have classified footage—perhaps from gun cameras or reconnaissance cameras—on file that UFO investigators would find extremely interesting. It's also almost a certainty the military has recorded radar signatures of UFOs (just as civilian radar stations occasionally do) and I'd further speculate that there are literally hours of plane-to-plane and plane-to-ground recordings of pilots talking about UFOs as well, some of which may even involve NASA spacecraft. That being said, however, if the military does know more about UFOs than it's letting on, why won't it tell us what it knows?

There are two likely scenarios that make sense: first, some of the evidence for UFOs may have been acquired using secret, state-of-the-art technology; to release the material, then, would compromise the sensitive nature—and even the existence—of this technology. In essence, how do you release pictures of a UFO taken by your newest high-resolution reconnaissance cameras without revealing to a potential enemy what extreme level of definition these cameras are capable of? A big part of military intelligence, after all, is not just in knowing what the enemy has, but in keeping the enemy from knowing what you have (and how well it works).

The second and probably more all-encompassing rationale for the military's silence, however, likely has more to do with its naturally secretive nature than anything else, especially regarding things it does not understand and cannot explain. For the military to tell all it knows would be to admit it has no control over its own airspace (an important concern, especially during the earliest years of the Cold War), which is not a good thing for any superpower to have to admit. Additionally, there is public reaction to take into consideration. Ufologists generally reject the notion that the general public would panic if the military admitted that our planet was being observed by some extraterrestrial civilization, believing instead that the populace has become so used to the idea of aliens that the revelation would come as little surprise. However, such a presumption fails to take into account human nature. As discussed earlier, while some people would accept the presence of extraterrestrials calmly (and perhaps even joyfully), many others would not. Consider that there are hundreds of millions or even billions of people around the world who have never given the prospect of extraterrestrials serious thought (or who do not believe in them at all), as well as apocalyptic religious sects that might easily interpret the existence of extraterrestrials in purely religious contexts, thereby possibly igniting a sort of "doomsday" response within their ranks. Even if only a tiny fraction of the populace reacted in fear and panic, that would still constitute tens of millions of people worldwide and place a huge strain on the world's police and military forces, as well as pose a major threat to the stability of many governments.

However, there could be another, more prosaic reason that the military doesn't come forward with what it knows, and that may be as simple as the prospect that many in positions of authority aren't convinced of the existence of UFOs themselves and so tend to ignore them. After all, the flow of information is often controlled by only a few people at the top, and if those people either don't believe in UFOs or fear for their careers if they became too accommodating about what they know, there is little chance that the admission of an incident—much less the details of it—will be released to the general public. This isn't evidence of some larger conspiracy of silence, however, but simply basic human nature.

To better illustrate how this could happen, let's imagine a scenario in which an unidentified target shows up on a radar scope at some military installation somewhere, and after repeated attempts to contact and identify the object have proven unsuccessful, a fighter is dispatched to check the object out. The pilot, upon arriving at the proper coordinates, reports the presence of a massive, brightly lit triangular object and promptly gives chase, only to find that the object quickly accelerates to Mach speeds and begins a series of maneuvers beyond his ability to match. After a few minutes of playing a one-sided game of cat-and-mouse, the mysterious object easily outdistances the fighter until it is lost from view, and after repeated attempts to relocate the target object prove futile, the pilot is told to return to base. After being questioned by the base's senior intelligence officers—and, perhaps, by the base commander himself—any camera footage, radar recordings, and ground-to-air communications recordings are impounded pending further investigation, and all participants in the event are sworn to secrecy under threat of court-martial.

Now the base commander—let's call him Colonel Jones—finds the footage and tapes compelling and passes them up the chain of command for further action. Unfortunately, his efforts encounter a roadblock in the form of his regional commander, whom we'll refer to as General Smith. Unlike Colonel Jones, General Smith, being something of a hardcore skeptic on the entire subject of UFOs, assumes the incident to have been some minor event that has been exaggerated out of proportion—probably the result of inexperience on the part of a young pilot and misidentification on the part of some over-caffeinated air traffic controllers. Further, since the incident did not result in death or damage to U.S. personnel or property, General Smith is under no obligation to do more than look at the report and recommend whatever action he deems appropriate. As such, perhaps more concerned with his own career than with the possibility that extraterrestrials are racing around his airspace, he has it shuffled off to some lower level adjutant to file and largely forgets about it.

Of course, Colonel Jones and everyone else involved in the incident eventually begins to wonder what became of the report, but the colonel—who is hoping to make general himself one day—doesn't push the issue. Weeks turn into months, and the incident soon begins to fade in urgency as well as from memory until eventually the whole affair is largely forgotten (or, at best, relegated to the status of an anecdote). Eventually, both Colonel Jones and General Smith move on, and the pilot and the other personnel involved in the incident are reassigned as part of the natural progression of their careers and the entire incident is effectively closed. Even if the participants choose to talk about the incident years later (after they have left the service), nothing remains but mere stories; the camera footage or air-to-ground communication tapes may still exist somewhere, but being classified ensures that they will remain buried in the Air Force's vast bureaucracy, permitting the whole affair to die a natural death.

I suppose it's possible, however, that such an incident, possessing so much solid evidence as it does, might garner some interest within the hierarchy of the military, but even should it be more carefully investigated, there is little that could be done with it.

Being a one-time incident that did not result in loss of life or property, at best it might be filed away with the small number of cases left unsolved to become another in a litany of "strange but true" stories, whispered to have some supporting evidence locked away somewhere, that have become the hallmark of the UFO controversy over the years.

I suspect this scenario is played out more often than not, and it would explain why the military—and the government in general—has been less than helpful in shedding light on the issue. It's not that there is some well-orchestrated conspiracy to suppress evidence of extraterrestrials afoot, but rather a natural skepticism and casualness about the entire issue that is at fault. Conspiracies are notoriously difficult to maintain; indifference, on the other hand, is effortless.

A Covert Government?

Some ufologists maintain that it's not our government that is attempting to keep the presence of aliens a secret, but rather a type of "shadow government" that is behind all the secrecy, with our own government playing either a minor role in the affair or being unwitting dupes of some international cabal. Perhaps no one has articulated this concept better than Dr. Steven Greer and his CSETI group, who maintain that, among other things, there is a massive alliance of evil industrialists intent on keeping alien technology—especially free-energy systems[21]—from the public in an effort to maintain their fossil-fuel based energy monopoly, and that this group remains beyond the reach of the United States gov-

---

21. Greer's group, for example, maintains that antigravitation propulsion and faster-than-light technology has been available to us since the 1950s thanks to reverse engineering the Roswell disk. However, the idea doesn't make sense from an economic standpoint: if such a group did possess an antigravity propulsion system, for example—as Greer maintains—such a technology would be worth far more than all the oil profits the world might ever realize. I'd imagine the temptation to steal this technology or sell it would be irresistible, especially to a group that supposedly operates on such shaky ethical and moral grounds to begin with.

ernment or any of its security or intelligence arms. He even suggests that many past U.S. presidents and CIA directors have been repeatedly rebuffed in their efforts to get to the truth about UFOs as a result of the efforts of this organization. Even more extraordinary, Greer's group also maintains that this cabal has manufactured fake UFOs to mislead the public about their true intent in an effort to start an intergalactic war with our peaceful friends from the stars, and has even created fake aliens (it's not clear whether these are small guys in suits, genetically created organisms, or robots of some kind) designed to make the public afraid of extraterrestrials by staging hoaxed alien abductions. Greer even implies that this group was responsible for the deaths of JFK and Marilyn Monroe, along with other public and private figures who were on the verge of spilling the beans about what they knew and had to be silenced.

While it is beyond the scope of this book to answer each charge in turn—and recognizing that not all ufologists who support the possibility of a "shadow government" go to such extremes—it is enough to say that such a possibility is even more remote than a government conspiracy, and for one good reason: an established government at least has the financial resources and security apparatus required to maintain some degree of secrecy about its activities, but a loose confederation of billionaire industrialists and rogue military officers would be almost impossible to sustain for any length of time. Operating outside the boundaries of the law would make such a group a very serious threat to any established government, making it a priority target for various intelligence agencies. The idea that it could survive such scrutiny for long is hard to imagine (unless, of course, it is operating under the auspices of the government, which is another issue entirely).

Further, it is unclear how such an organization could sustain itself for any length of time. Operationally, such a group would run more like an international drug cartel than a shadow government, with the various egos jockeying for power and attempting to destroy their competition through whatever means possible, making it almost a certainty that it would ultimately splinter into competing groups, each battling for dominance. In the end, such infighting couldn't help but tear the organization—regardless of how well-funded or organized it might be—to pieces, making it especially vulnerable to government prosecution. As such, the possibility of a covert government being able to operate outside the confines of the law, and being able to have done so for fifty years without a major defection, is more the stuff of James Bond movies than anything approaching reality.

The Potential Value of Disclosure

One aspect of the entire government cover-up scenario rarely considered by hardcore conspiracists is the potential benefits the government might enjoy were it to disclose all that it did know about UFOs. While there are several good reasons for wanting to continue withholding information—discussed in some detail already—there are also some good reasons to go public, the most self-evident being the impact such disclosure would have on the military's (and, by default, NASA's) research and development budget. Imagine if the government—perhaps working in coordination with senior scientists from NASA—were to go public with the news that extraterrestrials were observing our planet from high Earth orbit. Almost overnight, NASA's budget would quadruple as the public demanded that we attempt to make contact with these beings. The military might benefit as well by seeing an increase in funding by those leery of these beings' possible intentions, and the government itself would benefit from the increased goodwill it would acquire by finally being forthcoming and truthful about what it knows. I should imagine it would change the entire dynamics of our culture in many ways as well—most of them very positive: cooperation among industrialized nations, especially with regard to space exploration, would increase dramatically, and I suspect there would be positive fallout in the aftermath of how people view our place in the cosmos. Would the old paradigms mean as much as before—the quest for land, power, resources, the constant tension between the world's religions, the political tug of war our planet has been going through for centuries—if we saw ourselves as simply one struggling civilization adrift in a sea of such civilizations? It's difficult to say for certain, but if the government really wanted to reshuffle the deck, so to speak, in terms of the way we see it and the world in general, I can't imagine a more effective way of doing that than acknowledging that we are not alone in the universe. How could "business" possibly continue as usual under such a new paradigm?

So why hasn't our government (and, by default, other governments) come forth if it has so much to gain by disclosing what it knows? Beyond the practical security concerns discussed earlier, there are two possible reasons for remaining mute on the subject: either it doesn't have enough evidence to prove anything or it knows much more than it can reveal. For the government/military/NASA to publicly acknowledge the presence of extraterrestrials would never suffice; people would want to know *how much* it knows—especially including details like whether it has recovered alien saucers, has reverse engineered technology (and potentially hidden or suppressed technology), and whether it possesses alien bodies, putting the government in a very difficult position. Is the reason the government can't or won't tell us what it knows because its secrets are so great that to admit even one part of them would be to threaten the entire house of cards with collapse?

Conclusions

We just looked at the possibility that government knowledge about UFOs might be being kept from the public, either through indifference, skepticism, or by design, but what are the chances they're keeping more than just the potential reality of these visitors from us? What if, in fact, the government is not only now, but has been for years, actively suppressing the truth about extraterrestrial visitation in order to hide the fact that it has actually recovered crashed UFOs—and even the bodies of aliens themselves—as has been repeatedly charged with growing certainty and great passion by many in the UFO community? It's an important question to ask, especially considering the tremendous repercussions that would result were it to be proven true. To do so it will be necessary to move on to the next piece of the puzzle and examine in some detail just how likely is it that the government refuses to disclose what it knows about UFOs because of the extent of that knowledge. More specifically, we will go to the very heart of the entire cover-up conspiracy and examine the possibility that our government—along with other governments—knows far more about UFOs and their technology than it's willing to admit.

chapter eight

The Great Crashed-Disk Debate

It has been suggested by many in the UFO community that the U.S. government—along with possibly other governments—has in its possession at least one, and possibly several, crashed disks, some of which are intact enough for study. Second, it is charged that government scientists are currently attempting to integrate the technology gleaned from these recovered disks into our own via a process known as reverse engineering, thereby explaining the vastly accelerated rate of technological progress we have enjoyed over the last fifty years. And, finally, there are those who maintain that the government also has in its possession corpses of several aliens (and possibly some living aliens in custody as well, though this is a minority opinion), which have been examined, autopsied, and whose remains are currently being kept "on ice" at a top secret facility somewhere for further study.

What are the odds that any of these charges might be true? Let's see if we can't cut through the haze of conspiracy paranoia and consider the question from the standpoint of science and logic.

How Likely Is a UFO to Crash?

Obviously, any debate of this nature must begin with the premise that it is possible for an extraterrestrial craft to crash on Earth— either as a result of inclement weather, an onboard accident or malfunction, or through design (e.g., being shot down). However, what are the chances that any of these prospects are likely, especially considering the level of technology we are supposedly dealing with here?

The earliest accounts regarding the Roswell crash of 1947 maintained that the craft came down during a violent thunderstorm, implying that lightning was what did the little craft in, but how likely is it that an alien ship could be brought down by the weather? While such elements as ice, hail, heavy snow, sudden gusts of wind, and unexpected turbulence have all been known to bring down modern aircraft, it is difficult to imagine how an alien spacecraft—a piece of technology literally centuries ahead of our own—could be brought down by anything as simple as an afternoon thunderstorm. Are these craft really that fragile? (In which case, we might be permitted to ponder how they managed to survive the rigors of space flight to make it to our planet.) The whole notion that a sophisticated spacecraft could be brought down by a bolt of lightning is dubious at best and should give the careful UFO researcher reason to wonder. Further, even if it were possible, wouldn't these beings know to fly around or over a storm rather than through it? From their vantage point in orbit, they should have a pretty clear picture of the weather conditions below; certainly, it should take only minimal effort to avoid any potentially dangerous weather, or so one would imagine. As such, bad weather should be the most avoidable hazard an extraterrestrial would encounter, thereby making the prospect that a UFO might be downed due to a bad storm extremely unlikely.

However, what if weather is not the culprit? What if, instead, it was human intervention that brought several saucers down—as some have suggested? In other words, what if our military has occasionally shot alien spacecraft out of the sky and then seized the wreckage, both to cover their nefarious deeds as well as to harvest the treasure trove of alien technology the downed vessel would contain?

Again, while anything is theoretically possible, this appears to me even more fantastic than the possibility that a saucer could be brought down by the weather. Clearly any technology capable of finding its way around the speed-of-light hurdle should possess the means to anticipate, avoid, and/or defend itself from the comparatively primitive weapons we have at our disposal. This was especially true of the reputed crashes of the 1940s (e.g., Roswell), when the military possessed only the most basic air-defense systems, subsonic jet fighters were just beginning to come on the scene, and missile technology was still in its infancy. Considering the hypersonic speeds at which UFOs have been observed to fly and the astonishing degree of agility they have repeatedly demonstrated— and considering the fact that even modern supersonic fighters have trouble keeping pace with these machines—the possibility that a 1940s- or '50s-era jet would be able to catch a UFO, much less bring it down with simple gun cannons, is almost laughable. Only a close-in nuclear airburst would likely do the trick, but such would be noticed (and extraordinarily destructive), not to mention invite a likely alien counterstrike. As such, it seems logical to assume that extraterrestrial vehicles have little to fear from us, even with our arsenals of air-to-air missiles and supersonic stealth fighters; the technological gap is simply too expansive. It would be the equivalent of us using Civil War technology to destroy a modern nuclear submarine; it simply would not be possible.

But could it be possible that we might bring an alien craft down not by choice but inadvertently—say, through something as innocuous as microwave emissions from a nearby radar station somehow adversely affecting a UFO's flight controls? Might not that explain some crashes, especially the earliest ones in which radar stations were known to be operating in the immediate vicinity of the alleged crash?

Again, like the lightning-strike scenario suggested by some, any sufficiently advanced extraterrestrial technology should be well-shielded from whatever external energies it is likely to encounter, making it extremely unlikely that it would be affected by anything as basic as a microwave transmission. The cosmic emissions a spacecraft would be subjected to in space are far more substantial than anything a UFO would likely encounter while in Earth orbit, making anything short of a laser beam unlikely to impact a saucer's ability to fly.

However, what if the government *does* have secret laser weapons that have the ability to shoot a saucer down, as some contend?[22] While such might bring an extraterrestrial vehicle down, considering that the first commercial laser wasn't demonstrated until May of 1960, the idea that the military may have possessed a laser capable of bringing down a fast and maneuverable spacecraft as early as 1947 is absurd. Additionally, there are simply too many technological hurdles to overcome to make even a modern laser do much more than "paint" a target for precision-guided weapons, and even these are limited in their effectiveness by the stability of the laser platform and weather conditions (lasers, for example, do not do well in rain or fog). The degree of targeting capability and energy required to get a laser to burn through a fast-moving aerial target is still decades away, making the prospect that an alien saucer could be brought down by anything in our arsenals today (with the exception of nuclear weapons mentioned earlier) must remain in the realm of science fiction, at least for the time being. And besides, even if we did have such a weapon, wouldn't a high-tech saucer have some sort of defensive capabilities built into it or

---

22. Some even maintain that we've had lasers since the end of World War II (perhaps using captured Nazi technology), which the military evidently used to bring down a number of "flying disks" in the late 1940s and early 1950s before, presumably, thinking better of it and wisely discontinuing the practice.

shielding it that could shrug off a laser hit? If they have been study-ing us for any length of time, they would know of our war-making capability and factor that into the equation—or at least one would imagine.

Finally, while it is possible that one day we may possess the technology to bring an alien craft down, there is another point to consider: even if we had such technology at our disposal, what response might we expect from our visitors were we to actually try and use it? Might they not respond with force themselves, just as we would were an alien saucer to attack us? Certainly, considering the likely massive technological advantages a space-faring race would have over us, I can't imagine how we might possibly come out on the winning end of such a proposition. It would be the equivalent of a World War I fighter tangling with a modern jet fighter: the results would be quick, predictable, and messy.

Murphy's Law

If humans lack the means of bringing an alien craft down, then, and the weather seems equally incapable of doing it, that would seem to leave only one possibility, which is the prospect of a UFO crashing as a result of an accident—an onboard explosion perhaps, or another catastrophic mechanical failure. Since we can assume that Murphy's Law—the time-honored adage that maintains that whatever can go wrong, will go wrong—applies to extraterrestri-als as well as it does to us, the possibility that an alien craft might explode or be forced to make a crash landing becomes somewhat more plausible.

But such a possibility leaves us with even more questions. First, since most witnesses describe UFOs as being relatively small—rarely more than forty or fifty feet in diameter—it is difficult to imagine how such tiny vehicles could traverse the vast distances between stars alone. It's reasonable to assume that such a craft would require maintenance and repair facilities much as our own fighter aircraft need ground bases or aircraft carriers to operate from, mandating that they would likely require a base—a "mothership" in modern parlance—from which to operate.[23] This would do much to explain how such tiny craft might be capable of making the trip between the stars (as well as account for the large numbers of UFOs reported over the years). I suppose it's possible some could be working solo (or perhaps are expendable, unmanned probes not requiring support), but it seems fantastic to imagine that such small vessels could possess the capacity to operate so far from home without some sort of logistical support base.

If that's the case, however, that means any saucer that crashed on our planet would not be alone, but would probably be a small part of a much larger contingency and, as such, would likely be missed were it to suddenly vanish. Assuming that such a disappearance would be of considerable concern to our visitors (who doubtlessly keep track of the whereabouts of each of their craft), the question could be asked: just what would the mothership do in such a case?

I suppose we could simply imagine that they would have no interest (or, perhaps, the means) of recovering the lost craft and move on, but such an assumption sounds more like an effort to dodge the question than a real answer. Obviously, if extraterrestrials are sending ships to reconnoiter our planet and assuming they have a vested interest in maintaining their anonymity, the idea that they would make no effort to recover the craft and its occupants is inconceivable, especially considering the profound consequences that would be realized if the craft were allowed to fall into the hands of the very "primitives" they were studying. Not only would it prove that extraterrestrials existed—thereby compromising any further studies—but it would also expose a primitive culture to a level of technological sophistication that couldn't help but be detrimental to its development, especially considering its warlike tendencies.

---

23. Certainly very large UFOs—some many hundreds or even thousands of feet in diameter—have been occasionally reported, making the prospect that smaller saucers have base ships from which to operate more credible.

Further, they might even be concerned for our safety as well. Much as twentieth-century technology might be to nineteenth-century engineers who didn't understand what they were looking at—such as a functional nuclear reactor, for example—what we don't know about an alien technology could prove dangerous. This would make a speedy recovery—or, at least, the complete destruction of all evidence—imperative, both for the benefit of our extraterrestrial visitors as well as for our own safety.

But this brings up another interesting point: if we did locate a downed UFO and decided to make some effort to retrieve it, what would we do were we to come across an alien recovery team in the process of doing the same thing? Obviously, such a confrontation would not be in the ETs' best interest, especially if they wish to remain unobserved, and it is hoped the military would be wise enough not to interfere with such a retrieval effort, but mistakes could be made—with potentially devastating consequences.

Additionally, what if it became apparent to our visitors that direct retrieval of their downed craft was not possible due to the high probability of human contact? Clearly they couldn't allow us to simply start carting the stuff away, so what might they do? The obvious answer is that they would destroy the craft or its debris before we could get to it, either by firing upon it with their own version of a space-based weapon or by destroying it remotely from orbit (perhaps by activating a self-destruct mechanism specifically designed to prevent its capture—precisely as we have done with our own missiles to prevent them from doing collateral damage if they should malfunction). It's even possible that an alien civilization would design a sensor into its craft that would trigger the craft's destruction if it perceived human encroachment.[24] It seems to me that such precautions would be the minimum measures any advanced alien civilization that wished to remain unobserved would

---

24. This would also be true of unmanned solo probes as well; an alien culture would be foolish not to build some sort of self-destruct mechanism into even their most independent machines, for the reasons just noted.

take to protect their anonymity or, at least, to prevent their tech-nology from falling into the wrong hands. Any less on their part would not only be irresponsible but could prove to be potentially catastrophic as well.

The Prospect of Retrieval

For the sake of argument, however, let's assume that, for what-ever reason, an alien civilization was either unable or unwilling to retrieve their downed disk and we got to it first. Then what?

It certainly wouldn't be a matter of simply throwing the thing onto a flatbed truck and hauling it off to some secure airplane han-gar somewhere as many imagine. I suspect the reality of something like a real UFO retrieval would be very different from the "clean-up on aisle seven" procedures most people assume. A downed alien craft would be an extraordinarily dangerous piece of machinery to recover, both because of the likelihood of an onboard destruct mechanism and because of the nature of the device's power source. For example, what if it has a matter/anti-matter drive and one of the technicians inadvertently turns the containment field off? Could get pretty messy, one might suspect. Further, the fact that it may contain the remains of biological units on board would also make it a potential biohazard as well, further compounding the problem. As such, tinkering with a crashed alien vessel without understanding how it works—and especially without identifying and understand-ing its power source—is the equivalent of giving a three-year-old a loaded pistol to play with.

Assuming, however, that things go well and the debris does not appear to present an immediate danger (i.e., it does not appear to be manned, is not venting gases of some kind, and does not appear to be emitting any dangerous levels of radiation or other poten-tially lethal effects), the next step would be to excavate the craft for further study. While many assume the best thing would be to immediately move the debris to a secure site for further study, that would not be the case. A *real* crashed UFO would not be immediately moved but would instead be incrementally recovered and studied entirely at the site by a specially trained and equipped unit with the expertise—it is hoped—to do the job right.

In fact, this is where the fun would begin.

How to proceed would depend on the nature of the crash. Since aircraft seldom crash in one piece—most tend to break apart in mid-air before falling to Earth or impact the ground at a shallow angle, usually resulting in wreckage being strewn over a large area with one or two main impact craters—we must assume much the same thing would be true of an alien disk crash as well. As such, we would need to imagine a scenario in which not only would there be a main craft to recover, but a large area that would need to be cordoned off and each piece of wreckage carefully marked on a grid map—a time-consuming and precise process but an essential procedure if one really hopes to understand how the craft operated. In other words, a saucer retrieval would be treated more like an archeological dig than an NTSB investigation, and would be a process likely to take weeks or even months to complete, with scores of people in clunky rubber suits slowly and meticulously working to clear dirt out from around the impacted vehicle and recovering the object one tiny piece at a time (while constantly monitoring for radiation and biohazards throughout the process). And if you think it might go a little faster if the thing landed relatively intact, think again. The fact is that a relatively intact UFO would be even *more* dangerous, for that would imply that some or even all of the onboard technology is potentially still functional and, as such, deadly if mishandled—something that would be less of a concern were it merely a ball of molten slag buried thirty feet beneath the surface.

Of course, when it comes to older alleged UFO crashes, it could be argued that the military wasn't as enlightened about such things back then and so might have been more rough in their handling of the material, though this seems doubtful to me. Even then, the process would likely have been overseen by the finest scientists of the day, all of whom should have well understood the potential lethality of such a vehicle—as well as the value of its technology—so this just doesn't hold water. Scientists tend toward caution by nature; even if anxious to get their hands on alien technology, they would still have insisted the thing be handled with finesse, making the recovery a long and tedious process rather than a quick and painless procedure.

Retrieving Alien Organisms

I would be remiss if I didn't touch upon one aspect of this whole discussion that has been sadly underexamined, and that is the contention—made almost universally by legions of ufonauts—that not only does the government have in its possession crashed alien craft, but the bodies of their occupants as well. So how likely is this to be true?

Like the earlier problems in terms of saucer recovery, the idea that the government might possess the corpses of extraterrestrials is equally unlikely, and for many of the same reasons. Just as it would have in recovering its lost craft, an alien race would have a tremendous interest in recovering the bodies of their fallen comrades, not merely to continue to hide their presence or for propriety's sake (they likely have as strong a cultural tradition about their dead as we do), but for an even better reason: to prevent a full-scale plague from destroying all life on Earth.

That may sound alarmist but consider the possibility that an alien—providing it were carbon-based and physiologically similar to ourselves in some ways (meaning it has internal organs, a digestive tract, the capacity to process oxygen, and so on)—probably would harbor bacteria within its body that could well prove not only to be highly virulent but also extremely lethal to us were it to enter our environment. While it's theoretically possible our immune systems might be able to handle an alien "bug," it's far more likely that any alien bacteria or virus introduced into our world would make the plagues of the Dark Ages look like the sniffles. Without the means to stop such a pathogen, it would probably cut through the populace like a scythe and leave millions—if not billions—dead in its wake. Unless we were either able to build a natural immunity to it in time or produce an antibiotic that could fight it, there would be an excellent chance that we would perish as a species.

Additionally, if a highly lethal and resistant alien microorganism were to be accidentally introduced onto our planet, there is a reasonable chance that the aliens involved would probably feel compelled to do something about it and introduce themselves so they might provide us the technology to survive their inadvertently introduced plague, thereby prematurely showing themselves before they had a chance to acclimate us to their presence. As such, it seems extremely unlikely that an alien race would permit us to acquire, autopsy, or otherwise study one of their own under even controlled circumstances, much less through the crude means available to us today. Further, it would be equally stupid for us to even attempt to perform an autopsy on an alien body if one did come into our possession; even the most sterile environment couldn't absolutely guarantee that an alien microbe—perhaps one beyond our ability to detect with our current level of technology—might not be accidentally introduced into the environment, thereby unleashing a biohazard of biblical proportions.

On a side note, while it is probable that some UFOs—especially the more massive among them—are manned, I contend that it is equally likely that many—and perhaps most—of them are not, thereby rendering the entire issue of recovered alien bodies moot. My rationale is twofold: first, most saucers appear far too small to comfortably house a biological unit (much less several of them as has often been reported) along with all the environmental machinery necessary to keep them alive. Second, when one considers the tremendous speeds and abrupt maneuvers UFOs are frequently reported to make, they seem hardly capable of being manned by any living thing; any craft capable of making the high-speed, ninety-degree turns UFOs have been observed achieving would be lethal to even the hardiest biological entity. Unless there was some way to compensate for the many hundreds or, potentially, thousands of gs such maneuvers would incur, any life form riding in the vehicle would quickly be mashed into goo. Further, it would make more sense for the smaller disks to be unmanned, both to avoid even the remotest possibility of an alien organism falling into human hands—and all the likely negative repercussions that would entail—but also to eliminate the possibility of cross-contamination should an alien inadvertently bring a live Earth virus back to the mothership. Considering our own substantial progress in the field of unmanned vehicles over the last two decades, it's not difficult to imagine that extraterrestrials—especially considering the extremely advanced state of technology we're dealing with here—would have the ability to accomplish most of what they want to do entirely with unmanned vehicles. As such, the chances that the smaller disks are manned with living organisms strikes me as extremely unlikely.

Intentional Exchange of Technology

Of course, these problems would exist only if we work from the premise that extraterrestrials don't want their technology to be compromised. However, what if I'm being presumptuous in this? What if, in fact, they *intend* for their technology to be found for whatever reason?

This brings up the possibility, as some ufologists have suggested, that ETs either don't care if their technology falls into our hands—which makes little sense—or that they *fully intend it to do so*, either as a means of seeing what we're capable of doing with it (in effect, testing our technological acumen) or in an effort to assist us in our technological advancement as a species. Some have even suggested that we've already been contacted by extraterrestrials and a "deal" of sorts has been worked out between us, with our government's ongoing efforts at maintaining secrecy being carried out in exchange for some of their technological secrets.

None of these theories make sense, however. First, it is inconceivable that any advanced civilization wouldn't care whether their technology fell into the hands of a more primitive society, basically because of the damage such an infusion of new technologies would do. For example, what if such technology fell into the hands of a totalitarian government that would likely use it to dominate and enslave the planet? Wouldn't the ETs who permitted such a transfer of technology feel some obligation to reverse the damage? But even more, what if a government decided to use that technology against the ETs that thoughtlessly provided it? I can only imagine how that would be received back at the home planet (or interpreted by other space-faring races in the area—an issue we will explore in more detail later).

The second hypothesis, that they are testing our abilities to adapt their technology or are actually allowing us to reverse engineer it in an attempt to advance us as a species, while at least possessing some rationale, is also pointless (not to mention extremely reckless); if they have been studying us for some time, they are already aware of our level of technological aptitude—perhaps better than we are ourselves—making the transfer of technology for the purposes of testing us a waste of time. That they may be permitting us to integrate their technology into our own in an effort to advance us as a species, on the other hand, begs the question of why they would want to do such a thing. Clearly they—of all sentient beings—would understand better than most the potentially catastrophic impact such meddling in the development of a primitive culture would have; giving human beings access to technology centuries ahead of their own would be the equivalent of showing the ancient Romans how to make mustard gas.

Of course, it is possible extraterrestrials could have more benign motives for helping us advance technologically. Could they, for instance, be doing it out of some sort of cosmic maternal instinct that causes them to want to help us "grow up" so we might be better able to defend ourselves when we eventually encounter the more malevolent races out there (much like giving the Indians the technology to manufacture firearms prior to the first whites settling in the new world[25])? I suppose that's possible, but if that were the case, why not either defend us themselves—if they're really that concerned for us—or simply contact us and advise us of the danger directly instead of "feeding" us the innovative technology piecemeal over many decades. If advancing us technologically is the whole point of the exercise, waiting years for us to successfully reverse engineer one of their saucers (if, indeed, such is even possible from an engineering standpoint—see chapter 10) seems a dangerously slow way to go about doing it.

Further, if an alien race wanted to provide us an opportunity to advance ourselves by permitting us to reverse engineer its technology, why do it in such a clumsy way? Staging a saucer crash seems an amateurish tactic (and one fraught with uncertainty; how do they get the vehicle to crash without damaging the technology within it to the point that it would be rendered useless?). If the intentional transfer of technology were truly the rationale behind this charade, why not simply hand over in private what they wanted us to integrate into our industries, which would also have the advantage of providing them an opportunity to explain how it works along with the instructions necessary to replicate it?

Finally, the fourth hypothesis—that ETs are willing to strike a deal in which they provide us their technology in exchange for unfettered access to our skies—is even more problematic. As discussed earlier, if ETs are observing us, they undoubtedly possess the

---

25. Of course, they could have an ulterior motive for wanting us to develop more quickly than we already are. Perhaps in helping us along, they create a useful ally in their own war against another conquering species (or, perhaps, they *are* the conquering species and they're simply seeking out allies for their own war of expansion). In either case, however, waiting for us to figure out how their technology works by reverse engineering their crashed disks seems to be a painfully slow way to create a useful ally.

technology to do so without our being aware of them. As such, it's hard to imagine that they would need our "help" to remain hidden. Either they are a highly advanced race that is fully capable of taking care of themselves or they aren't, in which case we would be well within our rights to question their competency as galactic explorers.

chapter nine

Roswell: Anatomy of a Cover-up or Simply a Myth?

So what are the chances that our government—or any government for that matter—could manage to keep the retrieval of a crashed disk a secret and, even more, maintain that secret for, by some accounts, as long as sixty years?

While most people imagine the government has the ability to keep almost anything a secret regardless of its size and implications, years of government leaks, whistle blowers, and general ineptitude demonstrate precisely the opposite to be true. While small-scale secrets and a few high-profile military secrets might be maintained for a time, larger and far-reaching secrets—especially those that involve the cooperation and coordination of multiple government agencies (each with their own agendas to take into account)—are almost impossible to keep under wraps for any length of time;[26] people wishing to cash in on their knowledge and others who

---

26. Some UFO experts point to the Manhattan Project as an example of effective government secret-keeping, but it must be remembered it was only kept a secret for a little over four years and during wartime, when security measures are often far more extensive and even draconian in nature. Peacetime secret-keeping has always proven more difficult to maintain.

simply have big mouths all ensure that at some point the façade is going to crumble. Consider that something as relatively miniscule as a second-rate break-in at Democratic Party offices in the Watergate Hotel in the summer of 1972 could not remain a secret more than a few months even with all the powers of the presidency mobilized to protect it; how much more so, then, should something the size and magnitude of our government being in possession of alien hardware be as quickly compromised?

To better appreciate the magnitude of the problem, let's take a moment to examine one of the more celebrated cases of an alleged alien saucer recovery on record—the 1947 Roswell "crash"—so we might better understand the difficulty keeping such a thing secret for six decades would entail.

Roswell Revisited

For those unfamiliar with the story, the Roswell incident maintains that in July of 1947 a "flying disk" supposedly crashed—generally thought to be as a result of a lightning strike—on a small ranch about seventy-five miles northeast of Roswell, New Mexico. The discovery was made by a local rancher named William "Mac" Brazel who, upon finding a field strewn with what looked like rubber strips, tinfoil, and bits of wood, and after hearing reports about "flying disks" generated by the Arnold sighting over Mount Rainier two weeks earlier, began to wonder if he had found something otherworldly and approached the local sheriff about the possibility. It's not clear whether the sheriff shared Brazel's suspicions, but he dutifully called nearby Roswell Army Air Field just in case it was debris from a crashed aircraft. This elicited a visit from the Roswell base intelligence officer—a Major Jesse Marcel—who arrived to pick up some scattered debris, which he threw in the trunk of his car and drove back to base (but not before waking his twelve-year-old son in the middle of the night to show him what he had found—a decision, one might imagine, that should have been at considerable variance with standard retrieval policy). Though initially reported as a crashed "disk" by the military[27]—the debris was later explained away as a downed weather balloon, and the case was soon forgotten—even by the UFO community.

The story would probably have remained that way had it not been resurrected thirty years later when Mr. Marcel—along with a number of supposed witnesses to the wreckage and the bodies of its alien occupants,[28] who were initially cowed into silence by the government—apparently overcame their fears and stepped forward to spill the beans on the whole affair. Claiming the weather-balloon story to have been merely a cover for what could only be considered the find of the millennium, the story grew in complexity and detail until today the Roswell incident has not only become the chief exhibit in the case for a massive government cover-up but also the incident against which all other similar crash accounts have since been gauged.

But did it really happen? Did a saucer actually crash in New Mexico one stormy night in 1947, only to eventually fall into the hands of the United States government? It is beyond the scope of this book to revisit the evidence for and against the Roswell story with anything approaching thoroughness[29] so I will not attempt to do so here. Instead, I will simply consider the possibility from the perspective of logic, hopefully devoid of the often emotional rhetoric the issue elicits from many people, and let the reader decide for himself or herself how likely it is that the Roswell story is or even *could* be true.

The first problem with the story—other than the obvious objection of how reliable thirty-year-old memories are and how credible some of the witnesses have subsequently proven to be—is that the entire premise is untenable. As we considered in some detail a

---

27. It's important to recognize that describing an object as a "disk" at that time does not necessarily mean that the Air Force considered it of extraterrestrial origin. The term was simply a catch-all phrase often used to describe any unidentified aerial craft.

28. The claim that alien bodies were also found came later and from others. Brazel himself never stated that bodies were present at the crash site.

29. See my bibliography section.

moment ago, it simply isn't logical to imagine that any alien species that possesses the technology to travel from star to star wouldn't also possess both the means and the inclination to recover one of its downed craft. But even beyond that concern, however, is the sheer magnitude of the subsequent series of events to account for, especially in the aftermath of what could only be described as the most significant event in modern human history.

First, we have to assume the government, upon learning it had a crashed disk on its hands, would want to keep it quiet—both from the Soviets (against whom we were fighting a cold war) and from the presumably easily panicked general public. Immediately, however, we encounter several problems—not the least of them being the fact that the local radio stations had already gotten wind of the crash and the military had issued a press release to the fact that a "disk" had been recovered. Additionally, we have several civilian witnesses to the crash scene: Brazel, his granddaughter, the sheriff, and perhaps a few others. Of course, these people could be silenced either through intimidation or by appealing to their sense of patriotism; more difficult to control, however, would have been the dozens of soldiers supposedly sent from the nearby base at Roswell to recover the wreckage—and the alien corpses—along with the senior officers at the base and their superiors further up the chain of command who knew what was happening. The enlisted men and junior officers could be threatened with court-martial and imprisonment if they said anything (at least, until they left the service), while the senior officers, already inclined to follow orders by nature—and to ensure their continued advancement—would remain quiet. However, there's also the air crew of the plane that flies the saucer wreckage and aliens out of the area, along with the security people who will be in charge of its storage and security for an indefinite period of time. Then there are the various scientists, engineers, biologists, physicists, pathologists, metallurgists, and others who will study the craft—and its occupants, it is assumed—over the next few months to take into account, and, of course, the many

CIA, FBI, NSA, and other government agents required to maintain the overall veil of secrecy over the whole affair and come up with an appropriate cover story (these would be the people behind the Project Mogul explanation, one assumes).

Finally, this stuff is going to go all the way up the chain of command to the Joint Chiefs of Staff and, one would assume, the president himself. As you can see, then, within a few weeks literally hundreds of people will have played some role in the Roswell crash and its subsequent investigation and cover-up—a number that will grow into the thousands over the ensuing decades as others are brought into the loop to replace retiring officials and scientists.

See the problem here? Like a series of ever-expanding concentric circles, awareness of the recovered device grows exponentially as new people are told of the craft (which would be essential as personnel retire and others are brought in to replace them), making it practically a certainty that, in the end, a veritable legion of military, scientific, security, and intelligence personnel would know about the Roswell disk. Even if most of the participants remained silent either out of a sense of duty or by fear, with so many people involved, wouldn't a few "leaks in the dam" eventually appear—especially years later when many of the key players are retired and no longer worried about reprisals (or, perhaps, hopeful of making a name for themselves before they die)? If human nature is any indicator, I don't see how there wouldn't be many dozens of senior government officials and scientists with firsthand knowledge of the Roswell wreckage talking about it today, especially sixty years after the fact.

Of course, ufologists maintain that some *have* come forward to tell what they know, but to date these have been relatively minor players in the affair (mostly civilian "eyewitnesses" to the crash site), many of whom later changed their stories or were subsequently proven to have fabricated their accounts. Never has a high-level Pentagon official, senior credentialed scientist, or government agent known to have been intricately involved in top-secret government research during the 1940s and 1950s ever come forward to blow the whistle on the whole affair, even when doing so would gain them much in terms of fame (and, potentially, fortune).[30]

But wouldn't such people be putting their lives in jeopardy if they came forward, or, at a minimum, taking the risk of being maliciously attacked by government disinformation experts and ridiculed into silence? While revealing closely held government secrets is always risky, it seems that going public with the information would be the *best* way to guarantee one's safety, for suddenly nothing could happen to the whistle blower that wouldn't immediately bring suspicion upon the government. Further, it is assumed anyone who did come forward would be able to produce documentation or possess other evidence to demonstrate their story to be more than just a fable. A single retired general with a folder full of stolen documents, photographs, schematics, and autopsy reports would do the trick and while, yes, it would be technically illegal to do so, it's hard to imagine the government being able to put the man behind bars once everything was made public. Were Roswell true—and even a few of the many other reported saucer recoveries equally factual—there must be literally hundreds of "ticking bombs" out there with the knowledge and wherewithal to blow the lid off the whole affair. The fact that it hasn't happened yet, especially considering the large number of retired participants who are no longer on the government dole or are too old to care, suggests that there is nothing being hidden. Either that, or it is evidence that no matter how incompetent our government may be in every other aspect of its performance, keeping the lid on UFOs is the only area in which it excels.

---

30. Of course, what constitutes a "senior" official is difficult to gauge and open to interpretation. Some maintain that Lt. Col. Philip Corso and Area 51 engineer Bob Lazar were senior insiders, but even if their credentials—and stories—hold up, they would still be mere foot soldiers. The really "big fish" have yet to emerge.

Conclusions

Obviously, a single case doesn't prove anything—either for or against—the possibility that the government is hiding a great deal about what it knows about UFOs. In fact, even if Roswell turns out to be a complete fabrication, that still wouldn't demonstrate there isn't *something* to the notion that our government is hiding much; after all, the military isn't famous for its candor regarding what it does, so it isn't difficult to imagine that it might know more than it is willing to admit—at least publicly. On the other hand, this inherent reticence on the part of the military doesn't *prove* that a massive UFO cover-up is underway either; arguments from silence are always a very poor foundation upon which to construct any scenario—especially one as remarkable as the possibility of extraterrestrial visitation.

But let's put the substantial problems with recovering alien technology and the difficulty of keeping it a secret for sixty years aside for a moment and imagine for the sake of argument that our military *did* recover a downed UFO—or, perhaps, several of them over the years. Further, let's imagine they have been diligently studying these recovered craft ever since in an apparent effort to see not only what "makes them tick" but also to integrate what they learn into our own technology. In other words, could such be the reason behind the breathtaking advances in our own technological evolution over the last sixty years—a period of stunning and rapid advances that has taken us from vacuum tubes and short-wave radio to microchips and laptop computers in the span of a single lifetime?

In such a case, the first thing we'd need to consider is whether or not it is possible to "reverse engineer" an alien craft and integrate its technology into our own, as many in the UFO community insist has been happening for decades. To find out, let's explore the subject of "reverse engineering" in more detail to determine whether such a process is not only being done but whether it's even possible for us to do it at our current level of technical acumen.

chapter ten

Popping the Reverse-Engineering Bubble

The concept of reverse engineering itself is pretty straightforward: if an enemy or competitor produces a piece of technology that's clearly superior to anything you have, make every effort to get your hands on an example of it, take it apart to see what makes it tick, and then duplicate it yourself. In this way you effectively leapfrog past the design and testing phase and go straight to production with the device, thereby offsetting the enemy's or competitor's advantage and returning a degree of equilibrium to the equation.

Examples of successful reverse engineering are uncommon, but there are a couple of instances from history we might examine. One of the simplest or most low-tech examples was the British "jerry can" of World War II—essentially a well-designed petrol can the British copied from a German design. (Hence the nomenclature: "Jerry" was a derogatory nickname for the Germans used by the British throughout the war.) More high-tech examples would be the Soviet R-1 rocket, which was essentially a precise reproduction of the German V-2 rocket of World War II fame; and the Soviet

Tupolev Tu-4 bomber—again, an almost perfect rivet-for-rivet copy of an American B-29 bomber that had made a forced landing in the USSR late in the war.[31] In each case, it was simply a matter of taking apart something that already existed and integrating that technology into one's own, thus leapfrogging forward technologically and saving time and money in the process.

Reverse engineering is also sometimes used by archeologists in an effort to better understand or illustrate how a particular ancient mechanism originally worked. Perhaps the most famous example of this is the Antikythera device—a small mechanical device recovered from the waters off the Greek island of Antikythera in 1900—whose precise function remained a mystery to science for decades. Little more than a series of coral-encrusted gears and wheels, it wasn't until the 1950s, when x-rays were taken of the object, that archeologists were able to see inside the artifact, thereby giving them at last some idea of what the curious little device was for. What they eventually learned shook the academic world, for it turned out the Antikythera device was nothing less than a crude but effective mechanical "computer" capable of determining the position of the planets with remarkable accuracy. Obviously, this came as quite a shock to science, especially considering that despite being more than two thousand years old, it demonstrated a degree of mechanical complexity that wasn't to be seen again until the mid-nineteenth century.

Intrigued as to precisely how the ancients could have produced a functional computer and curious as to how the thing might have actually worked, in 1974 Yale science history professor Derek J. de Solla Price—an expert on the Antikythera artifact who had been studying the device since the 1950s—managed to construct a working model of the mechanism by using a process very much like

---

31. It's been demonstrated that the bomber the Soviets studied had a small aluminum plate riveted over some battle damage on its fuselage that was subsequently incorporated into the Soviet bomber, demonstrating how carefully—and literally—the Soviets copied the plane.

reverse engineering. Though his model was not entirely correct and was later improved upon by other researchers, it did demonstrate that something as corroded as a two-thousand-year-old set of bronze gears could be meticulously replicated using modern—though comparable—materials, again demonstrating the usefulness of reverse engineering.

The Need for Comparable Technologies

However, there is one big caveat to all this: reverse engineering only works on items that possess a comparable level of technology to our own, not one that is many decades or even centuries more advanced. For example, when the Soviets copied the German V-2 rocket and the American B-29 bomber, they were working with technologies they were already familiar with (and, in the case of the V-2, actually had German scientists assisting in the reverse engineering process), making the process far less magical than many might imagine. Additionally, the materials used to replicate these machines already existed, making the process merely a matter of copying an existing design, not inventing an entirely new technology.

Reverse engineering a highly advanced, alien technology— especially one as exotic and sophisticated as that which might be expected from a space-faring, extraterrestrial civilization—is an entirely different matter. It would take teams of experts (perhaps many hundreds or even thousands of engineers and scientists in all) decades to understand what function each particular mechanism on the craft performs, what it is composed of, what powers it has, and how it operated *before* they could even begin to determine whether we might be able to replicate it using materials currently available to us. To better illustrate this, let's suppose that a team of eighteenth-century scientists, engineers, and inventors found themselves in possession of a modern nuclear submarine and, using only the knowledge and tools available to them in their era, attempted to reverse engineer it. With no idea of what the literally millions of mechanical, electrical, and hydraulic parts that make up a modern submarine do, it would be so far beyond anything they understand that—beyond perhaps hazarding a few guesses about what functions some of the mechanisms performed—it's unlikely they could even begin to understand how the thing worked, much less how to duplicate it. Even something as simple as the wardroom coffee-maker would be a mystery to them; how much more so the ship's engineering, ballast, torpedo, targeting, radar, and reactor coolant systems would be.

Assuming they do manage, however, to eventually figure out how each system works (and presuming they don't get killed by inadvertently activating a torpedo warhead, get electrocuted in the thousands of miles of circuitry, or discover the unfortunate effects of radioactivity in the process), they would then need to integrate what they have learned into their own emerging technology. Considering the level of industrialization present in the late eighteenth century, how do they manage to replicate something as basic as a light bulb or an HVAC unit, much less a nuclear reactor?

Of course, we are more advanced and sophisticated than our eighteenth-century counterparts, it might be argued, giving us—it is assumed—a far better ability to understand the mechanics of an extraterrestrial spacecraft and a substantially greater capacity to replicate it than they would have had. However, this is pure hubris speaking: a machine that is capable of traversing the trillions of miles between stars and surviving the rigors of space is going to be as far ahead of us as a modern submarine would be to our eighteenth-century engineers and scientists. We might get an idea of what task some of the onboard mechanisms performed (just as our eighteenth-century predecessors might have been able to figure out how the submarine's ballast system worked, for instance), but in terms of having a clear understanding of how each piece operated and its overall function within the context of the greater machine, that would be far more difficult. It would simply be too far ahead of us, precisely in the same way our nuclear submarine would have been to men living two hundred years ago.

Further, it would be extremely dangerous to tinker with some-thing—much less dismantle it to see how it worked—without knowing what it was and how it operated. Just as it would have been for our eighteenth-century counterparts (imagine one of them unwittingly activating a torpedo warhead or turning off our nuclear submarine's reactor cooling system, thereby initiating a meltdown and possible explosion), playing with a technology we don't under-stand is a very dangerous game likely to have profound conse-quences for guessing wrong.

Additionally, we would be further hampered by the fact that many of the crashed UFOs we have supposedly recovered are badly damaged (in some cases they appear to leave little more than a pile of debris), further retarding the process. Obviously we would try and piece the crashed disk together—assuming we had all the parts—but even that would prove to be no easy process. It's not like reconstructing a demolished airliner in an effort to determine the cause of the crash; at least with a crashed airliner, we know where each part is supposed to go and what it does. With our hypothetical saucer, however, everything is purely a guess. Reverse engineering is difficult to do even under ideal conditions (i.e., the mechanism is undamaged and operational to begin with); to try and reverse engi-neer a nonfunctional, badly damaged, or demolished UFO without even the most basic understanding of how its inner workings func-tion would be not only difficult but, most probably, impossible.

Technological Infrastructure Problems

Then there is the problem of infrastructure to consider. No tech-nology stands by itself but is built upon the back of other technolo-gies—which in turn are dependent upon other technologies—to make them possible. In other words, simply understanding the inner workings of a light bulb is not particularly useful if one hasn't first grasped an understanding of how electricity makes the bulb glow and/or if one lacks the means of generating the electricity required to make it function in the first place, regardless of how well one may understand the underlying principles involved. Take any one element out of the loop and the entire process grinds to a halt. Our technology works because we have created the infrastructure that makes it all possible, an aspect of reverse engineering an alien technology that many of its most enthusiastic proponents often overlook.

Finally, many mechanisms must be made out of very specific materials in order to function (for example, microchips would be almost impossible to manufacture without the advent of plastic and other composite materials). As such, we would not only need to understand the precise chemical/element composition of each alien material, but then reconstitute the same materials here on Earth to precise alien specifications. To go back to our eighteenth-century submarine analogy again, most of the vessel would be constructed of materials completely unknown in that era; even if they had a complete working knowledge of how the submarine operated, the metals, plastics, composites, and so forth required to make their own version would still be centuries away, making any efforts at replicating our submarine impossible.

This, by the way, would not only be a problem for our counterparts from the eighteenth century, but it is also one science grapples with today. There are devices already on the drawing board that we could build now but lack the proper materials to make them a reality. A good example of this might be a hand-held laser capable of cutting through solid steel; we understand how such a device would function and could possibly even create the basic mechanism, but its power requirements are so immense that we are decades—or, more likely, centuries—away from developing a portable power source compact and powerful enough to make it work. I suspect anyone who tried to reverse engineer a sophisticated alien craft would run into the same problems when they found many of the materials onboard it to be composed of synthetic compounds centuries ahead of our own or operated by energy sources we lack the technology to reproduce. Understanding the inner workings of a highly advanced alien craft, then, is not only likely to be beyond us, but reverse engineering it even if we did acquire a thorough understanding of how it operates is likely beyond our current technological capacity—and may well remain so for centuries to come.

Extraterrestrial Assistance

Of course, many of these obstacles—though not all of them—might be circumvented if, instead of having to figure out the inner workings of a crashed—or even fully intact and functional—saucer ourselves, the ETs simply gave us the technology and even assisted us in developing it (much as German scientists did after World War II). Some ufologists, considering the aforementioned technological hurdles inherent to reverse engineering an alien technology, have even suggested that it is only through such coordinated collusion between an extraterrestrial species and our own government that reverse engineering an alien saucer *could* be done.

While certainly that would save considerable amounts of time and effort (as well as make the whole process considerably safer), it still wouldn't solve the infrastructure and materials difficulties we just discussed. Understanding precisely what a piece of technology does and what it is composed of would be no guarantee that we would be able to replicate it. Unless the ETs who gave us the machines in the first place were willing to completely revamp our technology to make it more compatible with their own—and do it in such a way that only a handful of scientists, engineers, and technicians would know about it—we are still going to be limited by our own level of technological capability.

I suppose it could be argued that if extraterrestrials were permitting us access to their technology in an effort to kick start our own technological evolution, it might be reasonable to assume they would provide us with only that technology we had the capacity to replicate with the materials available to us. This, of course, would be the *only* way we could benefit from extraterrestrial technology that would make sense from a scientific and engineering standpoint, but it still brings up several problems. Aside from the question of how such an egregious breech in scientific protocol might be interpreted by other space-faring races in the area,[32] how would such a transfer of technology—especially on such a large scale—be accomplished without literally thousands of people being in on the secret at some point? Even the most basic cutting-edge technology often requires whole teams of inventors and researchers to engineer it, even with outside help. The idea that even relatively simple devices could be successfully replicated and introduced into our culture without a legion of scientists, engineers, and the prerequisite security apparatus knowing about it strains credulity to the breaking point. It's simply too big a secret to keep hidden for long, and when you multiply that by the number of such devices being introduced simultaneously, the difficulty of keeping it all under wraps grows exponentially.

Conclusions

While the prospect of possessing genuine alien hardware is an exciting one to contemplate, the fact is that recovered disks, alien bodies, and teams of scientists diligently at work trying to marry alien technology with our own must remain either the product of some very fervent imaginations or a cynical attempt to play upon people's natural distrust of government and their love for conspiracies (as well as lack of technical and scientific knowledge). While I think it would be great if we did have a crashed disk in our possession, it strikes me more as a matter of wishful thinking than anything approaching plausibility to imagine that we do. Not only would we be unsuccessful if we tried to keep such a thing a secret, especially for sixty years, and be equally unlikely to be able to do much with their technology even if we possessed it, it's inconceivable that any

---

32. · It's difficult to imagine other species accepting such interference with indifference, especially considering how it might impact them down the road. Unless there is only a single race of extraterrestrials observing us and it is able to do what it wanted without fear of discovery or intervention, I should imagine the decision to intentionally intervene in another civilization's natural technological evolution couldn't help but be problematic and, potentially, even a source of conflict among the various alien civilizations interested in us.

extraterrestrial civilization would be stupid enough to let us get our hands on one of their machines in the first place—much less permit us to keep it. I could be wrong about that, of course, but if we're supposedly dealing with an extremely advanced civilization, I'm convinced that it is wise enough to understand the consequences of letting its technology fall into the wrong hands.

Further, there is the problem that each of the technologies that ufologists have suggested to be a result of reverse engineering—fiber optics, microchips, the transistor, night-vision optics, and stealth technology, to name a few—have an easily traceable and extensively documented history behind them. Even a casual look into the history behind the development of each of these "alien technologies" quickly demonstrates them to have very human origins, with the names of the researchers and the institutions and corporations involved in each step of their development clearly documented and—with the exception of some highly sensitive and still classified military hardware—a matter of public record.[33]

To suggest that many of our modern technologies are the result of reverse engineering alien technology is not only to badly underestimate human ingenuity and resourcefulness but also to dismiss the tireless contributions of the many scientists, engineers, and inventors who have spent so much of their lives developing these technologies. As such, it strikes me as unfair to those who did all the "grunt work" over the decades to so cavalierly ignore their efforts and dismiss their contributions as a cover for what is really just stolen technology. One can ignore almost everything in the quest to believe almost anything, but rewriting documented history and ignoring the remarkable contributions of science leaves one adrift in a sea of presumption for the sake of a pet theory.

---

33. Unless, of course, we assume that all of this is confabulated as well—demonstrating a conspiracy of such size and sophistication that it staggers the imagination.

PART THREE

Exploring the Alien Agenda

I've spent much of this book making the case that if there is such a thing as space-faring civilizations and if they are here observing us, they are doing so out of more than mere scientific curiosity. Indeed, if simple observation is the extent of their agenda, their presence would probably never be suspected, for they could easily observe from the safety of orbit without our ever being aware of their presence. However, we know that's not the case: their craft are occasionally spotted and sometimes even filmed; they periodically wander onto radar screens and entice Air Force fighters to chase them; and they even have been known to land and leave tantalizing clues behind. Some ufologists even claim they abduct people for obscure reasons and have made efforts to communicate with a handful of humans, thereby making their presence all the more evident—a strange tactic, one might argue, if their intention is to remain anonymous observers. As such, it seems apparent that if they exist at all, extraterrestrials are *permitting* themselves to work their way into our awareness for some reason. But if that's the case, then why—or, more precisely, *what* do they want? In effect, *what is their agenda?*

In the next few chapters we'll try to discern what that agenda might be, and whether it is benevolent or malevolent in nature. Additionally, it will be helpful to consider not only the *why* of alien intervention but the *how* of it as well; in other words, if an alien civilization were intent on making itself known to us and wished to do it in an inconspicuous way, what tactics or procedures might it use to do so? To find the answers, however, it will be necessary to consider the issue of interplanetary exploration from the standpoint of a highly evolved extraterrestrial civilization and what processes it might use in an effort to not only study its subjects, but make itself known in the most subtle and non-traumatic ways possible. In other words, we will need to *think* like an extraterrestrial—at least to whatever degree we are capable of doing so—if we are ever going to understand what they're up to.

chapter eleven

Planning Our Own
Voyage of Discovery

Earlier, we examined the various rationales an extraterrestrial civilization might have for coming to Earth, and we determined that exploration and study with an eye toward eventual contact was probably the most likely reason for spending the time and effort required to get here. As such, if we accept the prospect that extraterrestrials are even now doing precisely that, how exactly might that strategy look from our perspective? In other words, what would an entomologist look like from the perspective of the insect he was studying?

Obviously, trying to discern an alien mindset is always problematic, but not necessarily impossible if we consider what procedures we would likely employ were we to one day have the opportunity to study an advanced alien civilization. Of course, other races may have very different reasons for wanting to explore the universe and so may not be inclined to follow my step-by-step suggestions, but I believe there are certain universal constants in play that would make our exploration processes similar. If that's the case, then, we need only consider how we might put together an exploratory mission to another world and see if we can find parallels in it that might correspond to what ETs may be doing on our planet today.

The first problem any extensive observations of another civilization brings up is figuring out how we might go about learning about our subject without interfering in the very processes we are trying to study. In other words, in order for our data to be scientifically valid, we can't interfere in our subject's cultural or technological development in any way, but how do we prevent this contamination from taking place considering the difficulty studying any developing society would entail in the first place? Obviously, certain procedures would need to be put in place—protocols that should be as logical and progressive to an alien race as they would be to us—and meticulously adhered to, lest the entire process be compromised. But what would these protocols be?

The first and most basic one—and what we might even consider to be a law—is that, upon encountering a planet that harbors life on any level, it is imperative that we not interfere with the natural evolution of that world, particularly if that planet possessed intelligent life on even a primitive scale, for two very good reasons: first, noninterference would protect us from unforeseen threats such a world may potentially pose; and, second, it keeps us from contaminating our study. This basic principle was originally popularized in Gene Roddenberry's television classic *Star Trek* under the guise of something obtusely referred to as the "Prime Directive" and has since been elevated to the status of sci-fi lore. But despite finding its introduction within the realm of science fiction, it's an idea that not only has merit but would also be essential for any space-faring race of explorers to utilize.

As such, if humans—even at our still low level of sophistication—understand the need for such a policy, we should assume that any peaceful extraterrestrial civilization would recognize the validity of these basic points as well. Of course, that doesn't mean we—or, by extension, they—would necessarily use precisely the same procedures with each new planet encountered; undoubtedly each new world would need to be approached in different ways. For example, if the subject planet were assumed to be home to only simple life forms (based on all preliminary studies done from a distance), it would follow that a different set of protocols would be implemented than if it were a planet we suspected to be harboring higher life forms (and especially if it were showing evidence of possessing a nascent civilization). With the former, since simple organisms would not be readily disturbed by such an intrusion, we could use a fairly straightforward approach: perhaps send unmanned probes to the surface or even openly land on the planet to collect specimens. For a world composed of more advanced life forms, however, the process would be undoubtedly more complex and, as such, problematic—as we shall see.

But we are getting ahead of ourselves. First we need to examine the beginning in order to better understand the steps we would likely take in our quest to explore the cosmos—steps that we could assume any advanced and enlightened race intent on exploring the galaxy would take. I propose a four-step process.

STEP 1: Initial Long-Range Planetary Identification and Investigation (Passive Investigation)

Before any mission to an alien body is attempted, it would first be necessary to determine our subject planet's physical characteristics—size and mass, average temperature, atmospheric composition—all of which would be vital to determining the feasibility of further investigation and could be done from the safety of our own system. In essence, we would study a planet initially through spectrographic analysis and, perhaps if we are technologically advanced enough, through long-range visual inspection as well.[34] Of course, it would be assumed we would be studying a number of planets

---

34. This process may actually be going on already as we begin to identify planets in nearby solar systems, and it will only accelerate as the technology to determine the precise characteristics of these discovered planets becomes more refined.

simultaneously with an eye toward selecting the one—or ones—we considered most worthwhile to explore.

Once it was determined that a planet was a good candidate for further investigation—that is, it appeared to possess a non-toxic atmosphere and was rich in elements conducive for life—it would next be necessary to determine whether it might harbor life on any level which, again, could also be done from the safety of space by simply observing it visually through high-powered space-based telescopes (think of the Hubble on steroids) or through other as-yet-undeveloped technologies. We would be especially interested in searching for evidence of agriculture, man-made structures visible from space such as canals or artificial lakes, and even signs of possible cities, as well as listening for radio signals or other evidence of advanced technology. All of this, of course, would be done without the knowledge of any advanced life forms that could conceivably live there, thereby ensuring that the "Prime Directive" is in no way compromised.

STEP 2: Initial Surface Probes and Scans (Active Investigation-Preliminary)

Even the best deep-space telescopes are going to be able to tell us only so much about a planet many light years away, thereby necessitating that at some point we travel to it so we might take a better look. (Obviously, it is assumed by this point we have some faster-than-light capabilities, making such a journey feasible.) If we surmised that the planet appeared to be a good prospect for life, at this point we would send our first unmanned probes to orbit the subject planet and begin not only the first close-up scans of its surface but also the initial detailed search for life as well. In effect, this would be a preliminary "mapping" operation designed to tell us as much about the planet as possible without our actually setting foot upon its surface.

If, during the course of this study, life was determined to be present, it would be imperative to determine the extent and nature of that life before moving forward. If it were primitive life—simple micro-organisms all the way up to sophisticated multicellular creatures and large land and sea animals, for example—observations from orbit could proceed without any particular cautions being necessary (although we would still need to be careful as an orbital scan might fail to reveal the presence of smaller advanced organisms or potentially intelligent subterranean life). If it were determined that intelligent or sentient life was present, however, we would proceed in one of two ways. If this life was at a pre-civilized level, it could also be observed as before with little difficulty, though it would be important that all efforts be taken not to disturb these creatures or otherwise come into their awareness. However, if evidence of a primordial or pre-industrial civilization were found, the need for stealth would be more of a concern, as it's possible our probes might be spotted by ground observers, thus potentially becoming a part of their mythology. Obviously, this would be even more of a problem were the resident civilization showing signs of being technologically advanced.

As long as the civilization isn't space-capable, however, we should be able to continue our studies from orbit unobserved— especially if we have incorporated various stealth technologies into our vessels. However, we would still need to be cautious if they possess long-range observation devices (telescopes and binoculars) and possibly electronic detection equipment (e.g., radar) and orbital satellites, though even these should not be a problem since we would still be several generations of technology ahead of their own, making us capable of remaining unseen to all but the most advanced detection equipment. In such a case, the primary mission of our orbiting probe would shift from that of mapping and gathering biological data to one of observing the subject planet's cultures, belief systems, defensive capabilities, and historical record—at least as much as could be perceived from orbit.[35] These observations could take years or even decades to complete, and it would be imperative that they in no way interfere with the natural development of this society in any way while we continued our studies. During this period, it may be wise to assign the planet some sort of protected status—perhaps as a cultural or social preserve—precisely to prevent this from happening.[36]

However, what if we encounter evidence of an advanced civilization—perhaps one with an early space-faring capability? The planet would still need to be studied, so our orbital scans would continue as before, though now stealth would be of the utmost concern. Of course, it's likely we would have detected such a level of civilization from our long-range scans in the first place and have proceeded cautiously in our initial orbital investigations to begin with, making it less likely that we would be caught unaware and inadvertently detected. However, mistakes can happen, so extreme caution would be called for throughout this and the subsequent step 3 surface investigation period.

Note: At this point we might expect to encounter other alien species equally intent on studying our subject planet, which could prove to be a problem depending upon the nature and intent of the other species. If benevolent or neutral beings, this would perhaps be an opportunity to exchange knowledge of the subject planet or perhaps even coordinate future exploration efforts in order to reduce redundancy. If a less-benign species, however, it may be necessary to protect the subject planet or, if the opposing species is clearly more technologically advanced than our own, withdraw.

---

35. This would mandate that our probes have a high degree of computational capability and perhaps even possess a type of artificial intelligence to oversee and analyze it all, but that wouldn't be an unreasonable technological capability for an interstellar race to possess.

36. This would also be the case if the planet possessed no intelligent life as well, the main difference being that in this case it would be set aside as a nature preserve in order to protect its unique ecosystem for future study.

STEP 3: Surface Investigation
(Active Investigation-Intermediate)

Once we have learned all we can about the planet from orbit, at some point it will be necessary to enter the planet's atmosphere and even land on the surface for closer inspection if we are to continue on to the finer points of our investigation. One possible way this might be done would be to first "seed" the planet's atmosphere with thousands of tiny, disposable probes that would ride the air currents and slowly float to the ground, where they would explode or, perhaps, dissolve once they had completed their surveys and uploaded all data to our orbiting base ship, thereby leaving no evidence of their existence. These would then be followed up by more complex unmanned probes launched from the orbiting base ship, that would land directly on the surface to take samples of the atmosphere and soil. Presumably these devices would be sophisticated enough to explore the surface in some detail, possibly even possessing an ability to collect samples of the resident flora and fauna, which they could either analyze on the spot or return to the base ship for a more thorough analysis and cataloging. Of course, it would be necessary they sample the complete range of ecosystems and collect or analyze as many species of animal and plant life as possible (preferably in a non-destructive or non-traumatic way), thereby making this aspect of the investigation a lengthy one.

If a more advanced civilization were evident, our probes would need to be more subtle in order to avoid detection. They would even possibly need to possess the ability to self-destruct in case of a malfunction in order to maintain secrecy—especially on a planet with sentient life. In a case in which a probe fails to self-destruct and the chances of it being detected by the subject planet's sentient life forms is high, we would need to either recover it or have some sort of external destruction plan in place.

The existence of a global civilization would further dictate the range and capabilities of our probes as well. Obviously, we would want to minimize or even avoid the use of probes entirely in heavily populated areas and limit our studies to more remote regions of the planet. Acquiring samples of the local flora and fauna even under these circumstances would still be desirable—assuming it were done with care—though it would be important that all contact with sentient beings be avoided. In order to better understand the physiology of these beings, however, it may be necessary to acquire non-living samples for study, which would have to be done with careful deliberation and in such a way that detection is unlikely. Under no circumstances would living sentient beings be collected or otherwise examined.

STEP 4: Manned Investigations
(Active Investigation-Advanced)

Up to this point, all contact with the subject planet would be accomplished by unmanned probes, but at some point it's likely our scientists will want to observe the planet firsthand, necessitating a much more ambitious effort be mounted. This would undoubtedly require the services of a much larger orbital vehicle (or several) capable of maintaining large numbers of personnel for months or even years at a time, complete with extensive laboratory facilities capable of housing and analyzing the large number of specimens that will be collected. Obviously, such a large vessel, even in very high orbit, may still be detectable to a more advanced civilization, so the vessel would need to have considerable stealth capabilities that would allow it to remain hidden, both visually and electronically.

Of course, manned surface explorations would be undertaken only after an exhaustive study of the planet had been completed and it had been determined that the chances of cross-contamination were minimal (or, at the very least, had been fully accounted for and safeguarded against). Further, such excursions would have to be done in such a way as to ensure the minimal disruption of resident ecosystems, habitats, and in the case of intelligent life, resident cultures. However, even planets possessing intelligent life and exhibiting evidence of a moderately advanced civilization (say up to Earth circa nineteenth century) should be fairly easily studied at close range if all basic precautions are faithfully adhered to. Additionally, accidental interactions with the natives at this level would likely go unreported, hopefully minimizing the chances of compromising the study. Accidental interaction with a more highly advanced civilization, however, could prove problematic, necessitating that all observations be carried out only after we have acquired a thorough knowledge of the local culture's technological capability.

It may also be tempting at this point to wish to render assistance to our study subjects, especially if the developing civilization was in political distress or wracked by plague or other natural or man-made hardships, but such good intentions must not be indulged; to do so would not only destroy the value of the culture as a study subject, but it could also potentially alter its development in possibly catastrophic ways. I recognize that such a position is controversial, but it must be adhered to despite the distress doing so may incur. There simply is no means of determining how even the most innocent assistance might impact a society, so as long as our subjects remain unaware of our presence, it would be far wiser to let them struggle through the process themselves rather than interfere.

Aliens Among Us?

However, if I'm suggesting we might one day step foot upon a planet not only teeming with life but one possessing a fairly advanced civilization as well, doesn't that raise the prospect that extraterrestrials may have done the same in the past or even may now be doing the same on our planet today?

If there are extraterrestrials in our skies, it's likely they have physically landed on our planet many times, both in the distant past and today, but that's not really the issue here. What I'm talking about is the far more controversial idea that extraterrestrials have not merely walked on our planet but continue to do so on a regular basis without our awareness. Further, it is suggested by some that these beings are capable of taking on human form and of interacting with us without our being aware of their true nature.

Advocates of this idea—and they are legion—work from the premise that if extraterrestrials possess such an advanced level of technology, they should be able to operate among us without the use of an environmental suit. This belief is probably so common because ETs are rarely reported to be wearing any kind of "spacesuit" as human astronauts do (though accounts of them wearing certain types of silver jumpsuits are not uncommon). Additionally, since some extraterrestrials have been reported to possess an uncannily human appearance (sometimes even to the point of being sexually compatible) and of being able to speak fluent English or some other known terrestrial tongue, the mystery is further compounded. In fact, some have even claimed to have made contact with such beings who freely admit to their extraterrestrial nature (despite maintaining a completely human appearance)—claims not unlike those made by the first "contactees" back in the 1950s.

Unfortunately, such a possibility is extremely difficult to support scientifically. Probably the most obvious problem is understanding how an extraterrestrial organism would be able to physically survive in our atmosphere without some sort of environmental suit; regardless of how closely their home planet's atmosphere might mimic that of Earth, the chances of it being similar enough to make unsuited extravehicular exploration possible is highly unlikely. And even if, by some chance, they could breathe our air, there are other factors (such as levels of cosmic radiation, temperature ranges, air and barometric pressure, and so on) to take into account, all of which would have to be within their tolerances. As such, one would imagine that at a minimum they would require a breathing apparatus of some kind just to get around. I suppose it's possible that they might be able to make use of some sort of force field or atmospheric "bubble" that would both sustain them and protect them from Earth organisms (which might help explain why "grays" and other alien creatures usually appear naked), but such would be purely speculative. Still, it remains a possibility.

But that is the simpler objection. A bigger problem would be in understanding how an extraterrestrial might manage to make itself appear human enough that it could move among us without us being aware of it. Unfortunately, programs like *Star Trek*—and most science fiction that includes human/alien interactions for that matter—often leave us with the impression that many aliens are so biologically similar to humans (or capable of being easily altered in some way) that they are not only capable of surviving in our environment, but that they would even be able to interbreed with humans and produce hybrid children. However, while such a scenario works for the movies, the fact is that such an illusion can only be maintained if most of the uncomfortable science is ignored. The probability is that extraterrestrials, while possibly sharing some physical characteristics with us (i.e., being bipedal and approximately the same size, etc.), are far more likely to be as different from us as, say, we are from alligators.

The reasons for this have to do with biological evolution, which is generally thought to be a constant and consistent process throughout the universe. In other words, it is assumed that evolution takes place on all planets that harbor life and that such modifications take place via many of the same mechanisms that drive evolution on this planet. However, this doesn't mean that evolution looks the same on every planet; in fact, as each planet possesses differing atmospheres, gravities, and climates, each planet's evolutionary development would be by necessity entirely unique to itself. Further, evolution is also driven by often catastrophic events (asteroid and comet strikes, volcanism, global climate changes), which are also unique to each planet and unlikely to be replicated elsewhere in the universe. For example, had the KT asteroid—the event held to be most responsible for the extinction of the dinosaurs and in creating an environment in which mammals were eventually able to emerge as the dominant land animal on the planet—missed Earth sixty-five million years ago, it's quite possible reptiles would have eventually evolved to become the predominant sentient life form, making our biology extremely different from what it is today. As such, for an extraterrestrial to look similar to us would require that it take roughly the same evolutionary path that we did, which is, for all practical purposes, an impossibility. We might share a number of traits with an extraterrestrial race (i.e., symmetry, carbon-based, oxygen-breathing, comparable visual and auditory organs, and the like), but the odds of an alien looking enough like a human to pass for one in a crowd is astronomically low.

Second, even if an alien were externally almost anatomically indistinguishable from a human, the chances are excellent that its internal physiology would probably be very different from our own. Perhaps they would have an eight-chambered heart, for example, or a third lung or even a number of organs we don't possess (and, of course, their DNA would be completely different as well)—any one of which would demonstrate them to be nonhuman should they be examined by doctors. Of course, extensive surgical alterations might circumvent this problem to some degree, but how an alien DNA might be altered enough to pass for human remains inexplicable.

Finally, as discussed earlier, there is still the problem of cross-contamination to deal with. No matter how similar our appearance and even our physiology might be, the chances are excellent that the simplest strains of Earth bacteria would be lethal to an extraterrestrial (just as their bacteria would be to us), making direct contact between our species extremely dangerous. As such, unless they found a way to neutralize those effects—in both directions—extraterrestrials walking among us would probably prove fatal to both our species.

However, since we are dealing with an extremely advanced and likely exotic technology, it's always possible an alien race might find a way around these dilemmas, though I submit this is something more suited to the realm of wishful thinking than fact. Unless they had the capacity to encase themselves in some sort of aforementioned "containment bubble" or possessed the technology to create a fully human-appearing android of some kind—similar to Data on *Star Trek: The Next Generation*—the prospect of aliens roaming our planet—much less admitting the fact to a select group of "chosen" people—remains extremely unlikely.

To Contact or Not to Contact?

To return to our original premise, once a planet has been thoroughly explored, what would we—and, by association, an alien species—be most likely to do next? This is where it gets tricky, for now we are threading dangerously close to the question of first contact.

Obviously, the question is a significant one, fraught with ethical and practical considerations. If the resident civilization is still in the earliest stages of its technological evolution, contact would probably be inadvisable (and even potentially disastrous). Such a world would most likely simply be set aside and observed as a kind of sociology study until such time as it has evolved to a more technologically advanced level.

Once it has evolved to a more advanced level of technology, however—and especially if it has developed a primordial spacefaring capability of its own—the issue becomes more complex, for it is at this point that the difficult question of first contact comes up. Of course, the rationale for making ourselves known to our subjects at this point would be quite practical: if a civilization is advancing technologically at a fast pace (as ours appears to be doing today) it is reasonable to assume it will eventually acquire its own interstellar capability, making contact with other alien cultures inevitable. As such, contacting it under circumstances of our own choosing might be not only preferable but perhaps even wise, considering the likely negative consequences accidental contact would entail.

However, once the decision to make first contact has been made, what approach would be optimal? The answer to this question would depend largely upon the nature and character of the subject species: if they appear to already be open to the possibility of extraterrestrial life, contact would be less traumatic than if they had no such preconceived notions. In either case, it might be helpful to first discreetly bring ourselves into their awareness, but such must be done in a way that does not disrupt their natural development or spark a panic. Obviously, such would require considerable ingenuity and patience on our part, but there are a number of ways that it could be done—ways that we will explore next.

chapter twelve
First-Contact Protocols

It's not a simple task to initiate successful first contact with an advanced sentient race. One doesn't simply land on the equivalent of their White House lawn and request a meeting with their leader. There are multitudes of factors to consider, any one of which could have disastrous repercussions if mishandled. As such, and in an effort to better understand the challenges involved, it might be helpful to consider the process we might go through once the decision to make ourselves known to a developing alien culture were made.

First, we have to consider what purpose we might have for doing so. As discussed earlier, there are several reasons we might want to make contact—scientific curiosity, the need to expand our own realm of understanding, the desire to assist or protect races weaker and more primitive than our own—but I suspect the most likely would be the desire to avoid traumatizing an alien culture by making ourselves known before we were inadvertently discovered. If we work from the premise that each sentient civilization initially considers itself alone in the universe, the inevitable discovery that there are other races of sentient beings in the universe is bound to have a profound impact on even the most enlightened civilizations (and how much more so a primitive one?). As such, we would be wise to proceed slowly where first contact is involved.

But once the decision has been made—and it is being made for all the right reasons—what would be the first step? Contact the largest government? Broadcast a friendly greeting from space? Interrupt the news channels and announce ourselves?

None of these. Even the most subtle contact with a resident government would be foolish. First, if it is a fear-based society with a history of war (as is our own), its first response might well be to interpret any contact as a threat and respond militarily, with unpredictable and likely unfortunate consequences for all involved. Additionally, considering the natural limitations and the sheer size of most governmental entities, it would be almost impossible for it to maintain any degree of secrecy about first contact, again likely resulting in a panic. Further, if we approach only a single government—perhaps the most powerful on the planet—that may elicit ill will from the other governments that were not similarly contacted. If our own past is any indication, jealousy may be another universal constant that must be taken into account, especially when dealing with a planet made up of many nation states.

Of course, we could simply bypass government entities entirely and approach the scientific community directly, but that approach also has its own shortfalls. Aside from the same tendency toward jealousy, science does not work in a vacuum but is integrated into the public and private sectors as well. As such, approaching the scientific community would probably be just as chaotic as would be approaching a particular government, only there would be fewer mechanisms in place to maintain some degree of protocol and secrecy. For example, if a SETI scientist were to pick up a bona fide extraterrestrial communication on his or her receivers, the news would be public knowledge within hours, probably eliciting an, at best, unpredictable response from the general public (as well as from various governments).

Then there are the psychological consequences to consider. Clearly, the enormity of the news that they are not alone would have a profound impact on their society, much as it would on our own today. Though many ufologists laugh at the idea that humanity would panic were it to come to the knowledge that extraterrestrials are studying us from orbit, imagining that after decades of *Star Trek* and UFO reports we're too sophisticated to panic at the prospect, I suspect this premise is premature. Humanity, despite all its extraordinary advances in science and technology, and even religion and philosophy, is still extremely primitive in many ways. The existence of extraterrestrials—once admitted—would have major repercussions on everything from science and religion to history and morality, potentially sending the entire planet into free fall.

This would be of even greater consequence if extraterrestrials had made contact with us prematurely in the distant past. Imagine, for example, if it were determined that the Israelites had been led out of Egypt not by God but by extraterrestrials commanding them from the confines of a massive spaceship (hidden within a great cloud by day and a pillar of fire by night), or if Jesus turned out to have been a philosopher/alien intent on bringing enlightenment, or if Mohammed received the Koran not from the angel Gabriel but from an ET intent on bringing order to a land in chaos. The level of cognitive dissonance on the planet would be profound and likely politically destabilizing, with entire faith structures and institutions being shaken to their very foundations. How this might affect some governments—especially those heavily influenced by their religious institutions—can only be guessed at, but the fallout would likely be considerable.

But even if the ancients hadn't unknowingly interacted with extraterrestrials, there may still be other profound repercussions to consider. For example, what if after the initial shock had worn off, our subject civilization's next act was to clamor for us to "save" them from aging and disease by insisting we surrender our advanced technologies to them, or what if they demand that we solve all the problems they had created through their own shortsightedness and selfishness and are loath to tackle themselves? Further, might they not hold us responsible for all the great plagues and atrocities committed throughout their history once they learned we were present when they occurred and possessed the means to stop them but took no action? Clearly, first contact is fraught with as many consequences as advantages, mandating that any alien race who attempts it carefully consider the possible pitfalls of doing so beforehand.

So, how would we solve this problem, were we the ones trying to initiate first contact with a more primitive race than our own? I suggest the following six stages of contact, all designed to collectively "soften the blow" by allowing our subject race time to progressively adapt and accept our presence in a natural and non-traumatic way.

Stage 1 Contact: Observation

The first thing we would do is carefully observe our subject civilization in an effort to ascertain how it might respond to various approaches. Of course, we would have already been observing them for some time from orbit, but the thrust of these observations would be different. Unlike previous studies, we would not be as interested in understanding their history, traditions, and cultures as much as we would be in understanding their psyches. In effect, we would want to understand their fears and phobias, how they deal with change and adversity, and how they might be expected to respond to the unknown; in other words, we would want to understand what "makes them tick."

Fortunately, much of this could be done from a discreet distance by simply monitoring their information and entertainment broadcasts and observing how they collectively respond to what they would consider a crisis. Much of this information would have already been acquired from our initial scans of the planet made over several years—or, conceivably, even decades—but that would be only of marginal value; cultures evolve over time, making our understanding of what fears the subject civilization might have possessed in the past frequently obsolete in the present. If we were especially astute observers, however, there would be a number of consistencies we should be able to discern in our subjects that will assist us in subsequent efforts at contact.

Stage 2 Contact: Experimentation

Even the most careful and lengthy observations can only tell us so much about our subject civilization. To truly learn what we need to know, eventually it will become necessary to create a psychological profile of the entire species. How we might go about doing this precisely would be largely determined by the nature and level of sophistication the host society exhibits, and would vary from culture to culture. One way we might do this, however, is by manifesting some unusual phenomenon for our subjects to ponder and see how they react to it. In other words, we might leave subtle clues that we are here but nothing so obvious that it couldn't be ignored by the scientific community if it so chooses, but something that would still be beyond scientists' capacity to easily explain.

These "mysteries" could be almost anything our subjects found curious or unusual, from the subtle manipulation of their planet's weather to showing ourselves under carefully controlled circumstances, and then watching how they respond. Do they panic, scoff, try to explain it away, or do they instead look for answers, study it, accommodate it—even try to worship it? How does the culture integrate these mysteries into their collective mythologies and what impact do these mythologies have upon their social development? Does each new mystery make them more amiable toward the unknown or more frightened of it? What percentage of the populace is likely to panic (and what is the likely response of those who do) and what percentage is likely to accept it? This process could take decades to complete, but it would need to be done as an important intermediate step toward establishing first contact. Of course, there is the chance they will interpret some of our actions as hostile or even "evil," but even that would be taken into account when determining what sort of beings we are dealing with and what reactions they are likely to exhibit when we finally engage them.

Stage 3 Contact: Planting Evidence

Once we have determined the most likely response(s) of our subjects to the knowledge of our presence, we are now ready to make ourselves more evident without being too obvious. This would have to be something that clearly proves our existence to even the most hardened skeptics among them yet would be perceived in a non-threatening manner. For example, if our subject civilization possessed a primordial space-faring capability (one limited to their own system), we might leave some sort of artifact on a nearby planet for them to "accidentally" discover—something clearly of extraterrestrial origin (from their perspective), yet nothing that would be of technological value to them. This would, of course, not only be hailed as a remarkable discovery by their scientists, but permit the people time to process what the object means and how they choose to let it impact their life. Doing it in this manner would also lessen the likelihood of panic or fear and lay the foundation for more direct contact in the future.

Stage 4 Contact: Indirect Communication

Now that our subject species has had time to consider the implications behind the discovery of the artifact and have had time to process the fact that they are not the only advanced life in the cosmos, they are likely to expect and perhaps even anticipate further contact (this would probably be a period of accelerated space-faring development and robust searches for life on their part). As such, they—and we—would now be ready to proceed to direct contact. Again, however, this would need to be handled most delicately and also from a distance so as not to appear threatening. A simple series of mathematical codes (perhaps a set of prime numbers, for example) or something that could be identified as having originated from a definite and indisputably intelligent—and, hence, extraterrestrial—source could be broadcast from some point in space, permitting our subject civilization to be able to confirm our presence (though not our precise location). One assumes that this communication would be more readily accepted in the aftermath of the earlier artifact recovery, thereby hopefully minimizing panic. In either case, it is imperative that our presence not be perceived as a threat to them, which will hopefully be accomplished through the nonthreatening nature of our initial communications.

Stage 5 Contact: Direct Communication

Similar to stage four, once the subject civilization has had time to digest the fact of our presence and that we are in their immediate proximity, we are now ready to engage in more direct and less cryptic communications. These could be a series of short greetings (it is assumed that we have translated at least one of their languages by this time), emphasizing the benign nature of our contact and providing them an opportunity to respond if they so desire. Any mention of our previous or current presence on their world would need to be carefully omitted, of course, as it would be important they not feel we have been "spying" on them (despite the fact that we have been doing precisely that for many decades). This is the point at which trust is being established and nurtured, mandating that we not give them any reason to imagine us as being less than honest or in possession of a hidden and potentially sinister agenda. If all went well and trust were established, at this point a format and locale for direct contact would be agreed upon.

Stage 6 Contact: Full Contact

Full contact would be established, probably in space in order to reduce the possibility of cross-contamination as well as minimize the chances of them feeling as though we are "invading" their planet were our vessels to appear directly in their skies. We would also be wise to omit physically showing ourselves to them at this point (especially if they are significantly anatomically different from ourselves), though we could describe ourselves and perhaps provide some visuals for them to consider. Eventually, we would show ourselves to a select group of their scientists and government leaders and, through this contact, establish more permanent relations.

It's possible at this juncture that, despite the acclimation process, there would still be small groups—or even entire governments—that would respond in fear and panic to our presence, possibly even resulting in hostile actions being taken against our vessels should they appear in their skies, but we should be able to predict by this point which nation states may be most prone to respond in this fashion and avoid contact with them. However, our subjects may be unpredictable, and so the prospect of an attack must be taken into account (though we should possess the technological means to defend ourselves from such an attack, should it occur). Yet even in the case of a successful attack we would be wise not to respond in kind.

It would be imperative that beyond defending ourselves, no direct military action be taken on our part—even to the point of withdrawing if necessary until stability can be reestablished. Of course, it would be assumed that such a volatile contingency would have been anticipated prior to establishing contact, making such a scenario highly improbable, but one can never be certain.

Assuming there is no significant hostile response to our presence and contact has been properly established, at this point we would anticipate that our subjects would be extremely curious about us and would ask us numerous questions, all of which would need to be carefully screened before being answered. We would especially want to keep our previous dealings with their race a secret (though such information could probably be eventually revealed incrementally as our relationship developed into one of mutual trust), and we would also need to make it clear that we are not going to provide them with advanced technology or make any effort to advance their knowledge beyond the pace of their current development.

Of course, this could prove to be a potential source of conflict if not handled carefully, especially in those instances in which our advanced medical technologies might be vital in eliminating a plague of some kind (although this might be an instance in which our noninterference policy could be suspended, especially now that we have essentially grafted ourselves into their culture and if doing so would elicit greater levels of goodwill and trust). For the most part, however, it would be more advantageous for us to insist that they develop at their own pace, regardless of the resentment this could potentially invoke.

Finally, at some point it may be necessary to make our new friends aware of other sentient species in the area in an effort to prepare them for what lies ahead (and assure them of our protection until they are capable of dealing with any conceivable threats). By this time, however, we will have begun the process of merging our cultures to some degree, thereby making us a part of their ongoing development, just as they will become an integral part of our own future development.

Conclusions

The point of all this is that contact is going to be a slow and tedious process likely to take years or even decades to complete. Unfortunately, we are a species that always seems to be in a hurry, making me wonder if we will ever develop the patience to stretch out first contact this way, despite the obvious advantages doing so would entail. I hope by that point we will be able to see the wisdom behind such a gradual approach.

But what does all this have to do with our own experiences with UFOs? Am I proposing that extraterrestrials may be, in fact, working the very protocols I have just described in their patient quest to make themselves known to us today?

That's exactly what I'm saying.

Let us suppose that extraterrestrials are not only studying us— and have been for some time—but have decided to reveal themselves to us using the procedural standards I have just set forth. Further, let's suppose they are in the earliest stages of this process—the experimental phase (or stage-two contact procedures)—and have devised a number of tests or anomalous "mysteries" for us, all designed to study our reactions to them. If so, what could these mysteries be, and how might ETs be using them to lay the groundwork for eventual direct contact?

They're painfully obvious, once we start looking at our world from their unique perspective.

chapter thirteen

Exploring Earth Mysteries from Another Perspective

One calm, still night in August of 1972, two Britons, Bryce Bond and Arthur Shuttlewood, heard a strange buzzing noise in a wheat field near Warminster, England. Turning quickly to investigate the unusual sound, they watched in disbelief as beneath the light of a pale moonrise, "something" began pushing down and flattening the wheat before them, leaving a geometrically perfect circle some thirty feet in diameter. It was all over in seconds and as quickly as it began stillness returned to the English countryside, leaving the two men shaken by what they had seen. They didn't realize it at the time, but they had just witnessed the creation of the first recorded crop circle of the modern era, a phenomenon that has grown to international proportions since and remains one of the most perplexing—and mimicked—mystery of the last forty years.

Five years earlier and half a world away, another mystery that has defied explanation to this day first came to the public's attention when a three-year-old Appaloosa horse named Lady (subsequently misnamed Snippy in later newspaper accounts) failed to show up for her usual morning drink on the Harry King ranch twenty miles northeast of Alamosa, Colorado. Two days later, the horse's carcass was found in a nearby pasture, its flesh having been cleanly cut away from the shoulders to the ears as if by a laser. Later investigation also revealed the heart and brain were missing from the body, and a formaldehyde-like odor was emitted from the animal for several days after its discovery. Curiously, there were no tracks—animal, human, or vehicular—found near the body, but strange markings were found on the ground nearby: six indentations which formed a circle three feet in diameter. To this day what killed Lady and why her body was left in the condition it was remains a mystery, but not a solitary one; since then, hundreds of horses and cows—along with a few sheep and other farm animals—have been found in a similar condition around the world, making it one of the most unusual—and arguably grisly—mysteries on record.

Roughly that same time and half a country away, the Christiansen family of New Jersey reported a bewildering encounter with a strange man just a month after seeing and reporting a UFO hovering in the skies over Florida. Visited by a freakishly tall man—by some estimates almost seven feet in height—dressed completely in black and wearing a badge engraved with an unusual insignia, the mysterious stranger proceeded to question the family for nearly an hour on a wide range of subjects. Though strange in appearance and somewhat quirky in his mannerisms, what was most disconcerting of all to the Christiansens were not just his ominously bulging eyes and tinny computer-like voice, but the fact that wires were seen running down the inside of the man's leg that actually appeared to penetrate the skin. Finally, when the man left, he walked to the edge of the pavement where he was picked up by a black Cadillac—its headlights dimmed and windows tinted—that appeared seemingly out of nowhere to quickly whisk him away. No one knew who he was or what he wanted (beyond some personal family history), but his visit left all of them uneasy and feeling they had just had an encounter with someone—or something—not quite of this world.

And in perhaps the most remarkable experience of all, on the evening of August 20, 1976, four men—Jim Weiner, his twin brother Jack, Chuck Rak, and their guide, Charlie Foltz—all in their early twenties, were on a camping trip into the Allagash wilderness of Maine. Fishing late at night on Eagle Lake, each man noticed a silent, bright light nearby that seemed to be drawing near them. They thought little of it, however, until it pulled overhead and shot a brilliant beam of light at them, enveloping the four men and their canoe in its beam, before quickly speeding off. The next thing they remembered was suddenly finding themselves back on the lakeshore staring blankly out at the water, uncertain what had happened. After a fitful night of sleep, the next morning they packed their belongings and moved to a new campsite, the previous night's incident largely put behind them.

The men rarely spoke of the incident afterward, although it remained something of a mystery that continued to haunt them for years. It wasn't until twelve years later, however, that it began to reassert itself in their lives when the twin brothers, Jim and Jack Weiner, suddenly began having nightmares of being in a "medical examination room," where they found themselves being studied by strange creatures with large heads and huge black eyes. Finally deciding to tell their other two companions about their dreams, the Weiner brothers were surprised to learn that the other two were also having similar nightmares, which induced all four men to seek psychiatric counseling in an effort to get at the root of their apparently shared trauma. It was while under separately conducted hypnotic regressions that each in turn recounted the same remarkable story of being abducted from their canoe and taken inside the craft that they had seen at Eagle Lake, where they were subjected to tests and told telepathically by their "bug-eyed" interrogators that if they cooperated they would not be harmed. The revelation changed the four men's lives forever—just as similar experiences have changed the lives of literally thousands of people around the world who have had other encounters with UFOs since.

So what do these apparently unrelated events have in common? A flattened circle of wheat, a dead horse carcass, a mysterious stranger asking unusual questions, and four fishing buddies recounting an alien abduction appear to be entirely unrelated incidents, or so it would seem. However, if considered in the context of extraterrestrial visitation, they begin to form a pattern. Ever since UFOs first appeared on the scene over sixty years ago, a number of other phenomena have been associated in some way with extraterrestrials. The Bermuda Triangle, Atlantis, and the construction of the Great Pyramids of Egypt have all been suggested as having some relationship to extraterrestrials (even Bigfoot has been suggested by some to have been planted by aliens), but the mysteries most commonly associated with UFOs have been and continue to be crop circles, cattle mutilations, MIBs (Men in Black), and alien abductions. But while their relationship to each other and UFOs in general might not be immediately apparent, I believe that if one considers each of them from the perspective of how an observing intelligence might perceive them, their importance and the possible linkage between them becomes increasingly apparent. Let's look at each in more detail before we attempt to explore how they might conceivably fit within a larger agenda—an alien agenda—and what these mysteries might have to do with the possibility that extraterrestrials are preparing us for first contact.

Crop Circles

Perhaps one of the most intriguing mysteries on our planet today is what are called crop circles: those little—and some not-so-little—geometric shapes and elegant swirls imprinted in wheat and corn fields that have been appearing since the late 1970s around the world with ever-increasing frequency and sophistication. Although originally confined largely to England, today crop circles are a worldwide phenomenon that have taken on a mystique that rivals UFOs themselves in terms of cultural lore. These elegant and often beautiful swirls have even spawned their very own science—ceriology—that battles for recognition by the science community to this day, demonstrating just how serious these odd little patterns of flattened wheat are taken by many.

Of course, the initial assumption is that these agricultural oddities are mere hoaxes perpetrated by a few bored individuals anxious to demonstrate their ingenuity,[37] and in fact, it is thought that as many as 80 percent of the circles in England are hoaxes. There are even "circle" clubs that look upon crop circles as an art form and compete with each other in the creation of ever more sophisticated and elaborate designs in an effort to "outdo" the other. As such, it would be easy to dismiss the entire phenomenon as just a bit of fun or, at worse, some minor agricultural vandalism. However, among those who study these circles in detail, there is a consensus that while it's a near certainty that most crop circles are hoaxes, a small cadre of "genuine" crop circles are so peculiar in nature and structure that they defy easy explanation. Crop-circle investigators (often referred to as "croppies") insist there is a marked difference between a hoaxed crop circle and a "real" one. For example, whereas the crops in hoaxed circles show signs of having been trampled or crushed, the crops in true circles are intricately woven together and generally unbroken. Further, and even more inexplicably, the flattened stalks in true circles often show signs of genetic anomalies and some even exhibit the kind of burns consistent with what one might expect were the plants subjected to intense bursts of microwave emissions. Additionally, many who investigate these curious markings claim that true crop circles give off an unusual electromagnetic energy that can sometimes be picked up on instruments and dowsing rods, and have even been known to inexplicably drain camera batteries and induce dizziness, nausea, and fear—as well as occasionally feelings of euphoria, excitement, and a sense

---

37. In 1991, two men from Southampton, England, Doug Bower and Dave Chorley, came forward to admit that they had been responsible for a number of early circles, using planks, rope, hats, and wire as their only tools. They were responsible, however, for only a tiny number of the circles made.

of deep spirituality—in those who venture into the center of one. Of course, the physical and emotional aspects might be dismissed as the power of suggestion, but the fact that some crop circles exhibit unusual physical mutations on a molecular level or of having been subjected to apparent micro-bursts of intense microwave energy— impossible to achieve through any known natural processes— remains significant.

Even more curious, it is clear to even the most casual observer that while the earliest circles were largely simple ovals, modern circles are taking on ever greater levels of geometric and mathematical sophistication, demonstrating that they are clearly of intelligent design and not the result of some unusual natural force such as electromagnetic or plasma vortexes.[38] As such, to dismiss the entire phenomena as nothing more than clever hoaxes is simplistic; it appears that a genuine phenomenon is taking place, visible to anyone who bothers to suspend disbelief for a moment and take a careful look at the evidence.

So what is it that makes crop circles associated with extraterrestrials? (An assumption, by the way, that is far from universally accepted by all ceriologists; some claim that the circles are purely terrestrial in nature and have something to do with Earth energies.) The reason is twofold: first, many circles have been reported to appear suddenly in fields over which mysterious lights and other unexplained aerial phenomena have been recently observed; and second, the increasing sophistication of the circles suggests that they are the result of minds far more complex than those of the average hoaxer.

While the first premise is less verifiable, the second point does have some validity. While it is true that there may be a few individuals out there capable of producing the level of sophistication many of the circles display, such seems increasingly unlikely as the

---

38. The idea that some circles are the result of plasma vortexes has been suggested by biophysicist W. C. Levengood of the Pinelandia Biophysical lab in Michigan, but his hypothesis remains unproven and problematic at best.

levels of complexity increase (and begs the question of why these "geniuses" don't step forward to take credit for their ingenuity). Additionally, it is difficult to explain why these "superhoaxers" have never been caught, especially considering that some of the most complex designs would require many hours of work from dozens of individuals to create —all working in often pitch-black darkness frequently within sight of busy highways. In the end, it seems apparent that either *every* single crop circle ever produced—even the most remote and sophisticated—is the result of clever hoaxing (and that has been the case for decades), or at least a *few* circles are something else, either extraterrestrial—or, perhaps, paranormal—in origin.

If it's the former, however, we must consider not so much *how* extraterrestrials might create these patterns (certainly any sufficiently advanced civilization should possess the technology to create various patterns in any sort of field, perhaps by harnessing and controlling electromagnetic forces within the planet itself), but more importantly, *what* these extraterrestrial civilizations may be trying to tell us through the often indecipherable patterns they produce. It's unlikely they are creating them purely for their own amusement or as a means of demonstrating their technological acumen; if they are being produced by extraterrestrials at all, they must have a purpose, but what could it be?

Communication? Perhaps, but if they have been studying us for any length of time, why not simply produce patterns that we can easily understand, using our own language? Why the often indecipherable geometric shapes, random but carefully orchestrated swirls, and other often bizarre features? Certainly they must have more straightforward methods of communicating with us at their disposal than flattening wheat? And further, why would they attempt such an unusual method of communication, knowing that their original intent would very quickly be lost in a plethora of copycat hoaxes? Science clearly does not accept crop circles as evidence of extraterrestrial contact, so aren't all further efforts to create these circles one great waste of time on the part of our visitors?

Cattle Mutilations

Another less elegant and potentially more malevolent phenomenon noticed over the last few decades is that of dead, mutilated livestock whose wounds appear to be artificially produced by an apparently sophisticated technology. Ever since the late 1960s, cattle, horses, and, on occasion, even sheep have been discovered by ranchers with their sexual organs, eyes, and tongues removed with an almost surgical precision, leaving the remainder of the carcass largely untouched. Usually the carcasses are found in remote areas far from roads, and rarely are there tire tracks or footprints found nearby, even on muddy ground or in areas covered by freshly fallen snow, rendering the usual charges of vandalism difficult to support. Investigators have also noted that the carcasses rarely show signs of struggle, are frequently missing vital internal organs, and are often entirely drained of blood. Even more unusual from a naturalistic perspective is the fact that the carcasses—normally a magnet for scavengers—are left untouched for weeks and even months afterward, completely in contrast to what usually happens to carcasses left to rot in the open.

Of course, that's not to eliminate all natural explanations from the equation. Skeptics correctly point out that smaller scavengers—such as foxes—possess incisors that can leave remarkably straight edges, while the propensity to find the sexual organs, eyes, and tongues missing could simply be the result of scavengers finding the softer tissues of these organs more amiable to chewing than the tougher hides. Further, the apparent precision of the cuts may be a result of insects eating at the edges of wounds (which has the tendency to "smoothen" the rough edges of cuts and tears), while the lack of blood may be explained by the fact that blood frequently pools at the bottom of a carcass, making it appear as though it is entirely drained. Even the lack of tracks and the absence of signs of struggle might be explained by the fact that the animal could have died suddenly from natural causes (e.g., heart disease or from ingesting toxic vegetation), apparently giving the entire phenomenon a seemingly prosaic explanation. The problem, however, is that it would seem that ranchers and local veterinarians who have examined these carcasses would be aware of these factors and, further, it should be something that has been commonly encountered for centuries—not in just the last few decades. It is in the very fact that men who work with livestock for a living find these carcasses so unlike the many hundreds of others they've dealt with over the years that there's any controversy in the first place.

Deepening the mystery further, some ranchers have even claimed to have witnessed unusual lights in the sky for days or even weeks prior to the discovery of the carcasses (similar to the activity sometimes noted in the area of crop circles beforehand) as well as other unusual aerial activity such as noiseless, black, unmarked helicopters in the area. Some have even reported being threatened by unidentified strangers on the phone unless they remain silent about what they had found, implying an even darker agenda is afoot. Taken together, it all points to evidence of either malevolent extraterrestrials, nefarious government activity of some type, or a hoax on an unimaginable scale. In any case, something unusual is going on, despite the denials of government agencies and the military, and the work of debunkers to explain everything away as simply the work of hoaxers, predators, and insects.

What makes the cattle mutilation especially unusual is that we are not dealing with hysterical and easily frightened people here, but with multigenerational ranchers and farmers who know their livestock and can easily recognize the difference between an animal lost to natural causes (such as lightning strikes, sickness, or exposure) and one lost to predators. After all, their livestock is their livelihood, making one reasonably confident they should have seen the many ways animals can meet their demise. Further, it is not clear what reasons they would have for inventing stories of black helicopters or claiming threats on their lives when such did not happen. Either there is a host of ranchers and farmers out there prone to overactive imaginations, hoaxing, and paranoia, or there is clearly something more at work here.

Additionally, what are we to make of the lack of tracks—either human or animal—found around the carcasses? Certainly some of it can be attributed to the light weight of some scavengers and birds, who might well be able to approach the body (except in the snow) without leaving tracks.[39] Further, if the unusual wounds found on a carcass are the result of scavengers picking at the body, that doesn't tell us what killed the animal in the first place. It's fairly obvious when animals die because of lightning strikes or exposure, and a kill by a predator leaves considerable evidence of a struggle (and usually a partially devoured carcass). Of course, a high-powered rifle fired from a distance would do the trick, but that would leave an obvious bullet hole and a slug in the carcass to explain what had killed the animal.

This has led some to speculate that the animals were killed and mutilated elsewhere and dropped in a field, either from a truck or from the air, but both possibilities leave a number of questions unanswered. If from a truck, for example, why no tire marks (and why are the carcasses often found so far from roads)? If from the air, why is the aircraft (presumably a helicopter) rarely heard or seen?

But the biggest question remains: why? If it is some sort of secret government experiment (which would explain the unmarked helicopters), what is the purpose behind it and, further, why steal animals that could be inconspicuously purchased through normal channels and then leave their mutilated corpses somewhere they are sure to be discovered (usually on the very ranch from which they were stolen)? If the government simply wanted to test some

---

39. It is not always certain that tracks were absent, since often the area around the carcass has been compromised by the time investigators arrive, potentially obliterating any traces that might have been originally evident. Additionally, some carcasses aren't discovered for several days, permitting time for natural forces to erode any tracks that may have been originally present.

sort of new surgical laser, for example, it would be far easier for them to purchase an animal through normal channels, perform their tests at some secure location, and then dispose of the body by burning it in an incinerator, thereby eliminating all evidence of their experiments.

But the prospect that these events could be the product of an alien intelligence is even more difficult to comprehend. Aside from the same objections listed above, there is even less logic for performing such apparently senseless tests on the native fauna. Any extraterrestrial race would know the capabilities of whatever technology it possessed without having to field test it on livestock (much less leave evidence of itself on the rancher's doorstep) nor would they likely make use of primitive—by extraterrestrial standards—and conspicuously unmarked helicopters to go about their nefarious deeds. Further, the suggestion made by some that they are "harvesting" the carcasses in some way (perhaps removing the blood and certain organs and discarding the rest) doesn't explain why the ETs would leave evidence of themselves in the process; wouldn't simply vaporizing the discarded carcass afterward make more sense? The entire issue, then, consistently leaves us with far more questions than answers, just as it has for over forty years.

MIBs (Men in Black)

Ever since the first contactee stories emerged in the early 1950s, people have reported being visited by slightly quirky characters—normally dressed in black suits and sporting black sunglasses—who question them at some length about their UFO encounters and demand to be given whatever evidence (photos, film footage, physical evidence) the individual might possess—which is then confiscated, never to be seen again. Frequently these men—and they are almost always male—speak with strange accents and seem a bit odd; for example, they might be puzzled about how a timepiece works or fascinated with something as simple as a glass of water, while their cover stories of being from a local UFO-investigation organization, "the government," or some other nebulous federal agency appear contrived and unconvincing. They have even been occasionally known to threaten witnesses if they go public with their stories (threats, it appears, that fortunately are never carried out). But perhaps the strangest aspect of these people is the fact that they arrive and depart with remarkable suddenness—almost as if they are instantly dropped off and picked up mere feet from the front door. There have even been reports in which the mysterious visitor's footprints in the snow end abruptly just yards from the home they had just visited, as though they simply vanished into thin air. There have also been accounts of these individuals being picked up by black, 1950s-era Cadillacs being driven by "Oriental-looking" men, all wearing the same identical black suits and sporting the same identical sunglasses. It all sounds like the plotline to some B-grade science-fiction movie (and it was actually the inspiration behind the 1997 hit *Men in Black*), but dozens of such cases have been reported since the late 1950s, forcing us to take a serious look at the phenomenon.

So, what are we to make of these unusual stories? Mass paranoia? Bizarre *X-Files*-type government agents? Someone having a bit of fun?

Obviously, it would be easy to dismiss such reports out of hand as either hoaxes or simple overreactions to interacting with an unusual or "odd" person, but these encounters are frequently witnessed by several people simultaneously, making the case far more problematic. Further, reports of MIBs are fairly well documented and are often provided by normally reliable witnesses, so they can't be dismissed outright. Yet who—or perhaps more correctly—*what* could they be?

The most obvious answer—once hoaxing and simple misunderstandings are eliminated—is that MIBs are operatives from either some secret government agency whose job it is to suppress all evidence of extraterrestrials, or that they are agents of a "shadow government" or some other private organization designed to do the same thing. Both ideas, however, seem poorly thought out: would any such organization really operate in such a clumsy manner and act in such bizarre ways, and further, how is it that none of these "agents" have ever stepped forward to blow the whistle on the whole affair?[40] Plus, if their purpose is to suppress evidence of extraterrestrials, they appear to be extraordinarily inept at it, as evidenced by the many thousands of reports made each year. As such, I personally find it harder to believe that such an organization could operate for decades undetected than that extraterrestrials are behind it all.

And what of the possibility that MIBs may be just that: either extraterrestrials disguised as humans (explaining their often eccentric behavior) or androids of some kind (again, not quite perfected)? It's possible, I suppose, though neither explanation strikes me as being very plausible. Even an alien race that was remarkably human in appearance (a long shot, statistically speaking) or that could alter its appearance to appear human would be taking a huge chance by stepping foot on terra firma, both physically, in terms of potential cross-contamination, and practically, in terms of taking the chance of being captured, especially just to perform the fairly minor task of questioning witnesses about what they saw and issuing a few halfhearted threats. In other words, simply showing up on their subjects' doorstep and threatening them (or, in some cases, confiscating photos and artifacts) seems a decidedly low-tech approach to maintaining anonymity, and one that leaves a big "fingerprint" in the form of anecdotal stories.

An android would avoid many of these problems, of course (with the exception of capture), but would necessitate the existence of a profoundly advanced technological capability to pull it off. However, while these mysterious individuals' movements are

---

40. Another suggestion that has been offered over the years is that these agents are purposely acting strange in an effort to essentially discredit the whole UFO phenomenon by making those who report UFOs sound unbelievable. Of course, this still wouldn't explain why none of these agents have ever stepped forward and admitted their culpability, if such were truly the case.

sometimes described as mechanical or "robot-like" in nature, few witnesses report MIBs to be anything but fully human in appearance—even to the point that they have been noted to be sweating profusely. Further, if an alien civilization possessed the technology necessary to create an android capable of passing for a human, wouldn't it also have the technology to get what it wanted from their subjects in other, less conspicuous and less intrusive ways? Or again, as with crop circles and cattle mutilations, could something more be at work here—something that's happening for reasons we have up until now failed to consider?

Alien Abductions

Perhaps no element of the UFO phenomenon is more controversial than that of alien abductions. Ever since Barney and Betty Hill professed to have been taken onboard a UFO against their will (and largely outside their conscious memories) in 1961, hundreds of people from all walks of life have since come forward to confess that they, too, have had similar experiences. UFO researcher Bud Hopkins, perhaps the most prolific investigator into the abduction mystery, has documented hundreds of such cases, many of them extraordinary in their degree of detail and consistency, told by people who have no desire to have their experiences made public.

Basically, alien abductions occur in one of two ways. In the first scenario, as was the case with the Hills, individuals will notice an unusual light in the sky and pull off the road to watch it for a time, after which they resume their journey only to suddenly find themselves arriving at their destination several hours late and unable to account for the missing time. Afterward they may start having increasingly disturbing nightmares or experience other psychological difficulties, which eventually grow so acute that they are forced to seek the services of a therapist to get to the underlying trauma. It is then, usually as a result of being put into hypnotic regression, that they learn that during the several hours of missing time in question they were whisked from their vehicle to some sort of "ship" where they were medically probed by small, bug-eyed aliens (usually referred to as "grays") and then released—revelations that frequently turn out to be as traumatizing as the abduction experience itself.

The other scenario is nearly identical but with the major exception that the subjects are not taken from a car or while otherwise out in the open, but are abducted in their own home by "something" that awakens them in the night, either carries or "floats" them away to some medical examination room, and then deposits them back in their bed the next morning. In both scenarios, the memories of the abduction can usually only be recovered under hypnosis (although there have been cases of conscious recall) and the event usually results in the victim living in fear of repeated abductions. Some even report waking up from the experience with unusual and/or inexplicable scars or of having had "probes" or other mechanical devices implanted into their body. Some women have even accused their abductors of having removed a fetus from their uterus (or, sometimes, implanting them, only to have the developing fetus removed in a second abduction experience). In any case, the experiences invariably leave their victims traumatized and forever altered by their alleged encounters—traumas that often require years of therapy before recovery is possible.

Of course, science dismisses these experiences as either hoaxes, nightmares (or, more precisely, sleep paralysis), hallucinations, or the delusions of an unstable and/or fantasy-prone personality, thereby effectively removing the entire subject from serious scientific consideration. Noting that the subjects of alien abductions are frequently "eccentric" personality types who either consciously or subconsciously crave attention, they point out that the remarkable consistency of the stories suggest that these people have all been influenced by the same archetypes (lost time, probing of sexual organs, bug-eyed "grays") derived from forty years of abduction accounts. In effect, they argue that people already steeped in abduction stories (or at least aware of them through books and television) imagine themselves to have been abducted by these same "entities" out of a need for attention or to bring color into their lives, and do so by using the images of what an alien abduction is *supposed* to look like, taken from our shared mythology. They also correctly point out that abduction experiences have kept pace with our technology, noting that descriptions of the interiors of alien vessels keep pace[41] with our own level of technological progress.

There are a couple of problems with this explanation, however. First, while it is true that many abductees frequently display personality traits that might be considered "eccentric"—however one cares to define the term—not all do; many abductees are not particularly different from most people and many, in fact, had little or no real interest in UFOs prior to their abduction (similar to people who didn't believe in ghosts before seeing one themselves), leaving the one-size-fits-all explanation of science decidedly unsatisfying. Additionally, it is not clear whether a subject's eccentricity was resident prior to the abduction or manifested itself later, *potentially as a byproduct of the abduction itself.* Certainly, if a genuine experience, the trauma of such an event couldn't help but render its victim somewhat paranoid and perhaps prone to a wild imagination—many of the characteristics often associated with those identified by medical science as exhibiting an eccentric personality. It appears to be a question of which came first, the chicken or the egg; do abductions happen to people *because* they are eccentric, or do people exhibit eccentric personality traits *because they were abducted?*

But what of the inexplicable scars and materials frequently reported to have been placed in abductees' bodies? Science generally explains these as the consequences of a faulty memory; in essence, it is assumed that over the course of a lifetime a person will naturally sustain a number of small scars and marks on their body as a result of accidents or other forgotten mishaps (especially if they

---

41. Betty Hill, for instance, noted that the aliens kept their "star charts" on scrolls of paper—a primitive method of carrying charts but perfectly plausible for someone from the pre-computer world of 1961.

were relatively insubstantial to begin with). Then, once they are convinced they have had an abduction experience, they suddenly "notice" a mysterious scar on their arm or abdomen that has always been there but was ignored until the "abduction" event. Much the same explanation goes for the tiny fragments of metal that are sometimes removed from a subject, which some maintain to be alien tracking devices of some kind. Skeptics have pointed out that small shavings of metal or glass can be acquired quite naturally[42] or could be embedded as the result of a forgotten industrial accident, only to be noticed later in x-rays and interpreted as being of extraterrestrial origin—an explanation that is not as far-fetched as it seems: in January 2005, a Littleton, Colorado, man, complaining of a toothache and severe pain in the roof of his mouth, was found to have a four-inch nail driven into the front of his skull, the result of an accident with a nail gun several days earlier. The subject had apparently inadvertently shot himself in the mouth with the gun, but as there was little bleeding at the time, he dismissed the incident as a "near miss" and ignored it until symptoms later appeared. If the man had lived with the embedded nail for years without pain, only to have it be discovered in the aftermath of an alleged alien abduction, one wonders if it wouldn't have been assumed to have been implanted rather than simply the result of an overlooked accident.

Skeptics also frequently point out that of those metal fragments that have been removed from abductees and tested, none have shown themselves to be of extraterrestrial manufacture or particularly remarkable in any way. Almost invariably they turn out to be tiny metal shards of common manufacture that could be easily embedded in one's body unaware and remain inert—and, as such, unnoticed—for many years. On the other hand, it could be argued that if an alien race *did* want to track their subjects after their release—sort of an extraterrestrial tag-and-release program—they might be wise to use common Earth-born materials to do so. After

---

42. Tiny slivers of glass and metal, for example, can be driven into a calloused sole without pain simply by walking across the ground in bare feet.

all, what better way to give themselves away than by inserting a clearly nonterrestrial material into a human abductee? Of course, the opposite argument could be made as well: how would a simple shard of metal work as a tracking device? Neither position seems to offer a particularly satisfying answer.

The other problem with the abduction phenomenon is both the lack of the aforementioned physical evidence (beyond the subject's physiological or psychological symptoms) and the peculiar lack of eyewitnesses to such an event. Hundreds of reports of alien abductions have been documented—with many more going unreported, at least according to abduction investigators—making it difficult to imagine that not a single one of them wouldn't have been noticed and verified by independent witnesses. Highways are rarely entirely deserted; one would imagine at least a few people would see an alien craft descend from the sky and snatch a person from their car, while it is similarly remarkable that no one has noticed their houseguests (and, sometimes, their bedmate) being spirited away by a phalanx of "grays." It just strikes me as being a bit too obvious a thing to miss.

The other question that needs to be addressed is why extraterrestrials would even want to abduct average citizens from their cars or beds and perform all sorts of bizarre experiments on them in the first place. Common wisdom is that they are either doing so as a means of studying us physiologically or, as we discussed earlier, they are conducting genetic experiments in an effort to either modify basic human physiology or create some sort of "hybrid" race of human/alien, possibly in an effort to procreate their own dying species. Neither scenario, however, makes sense.

With the first hypothesis, it's difficult to see what more extraterrestrials might learn about us by essentially repeating the same medical procedures on hundreds (if not thousands) of essentially anatomically identical human beings. Shouldn't they already have a pretty thorough understanding of human physiology by now and, even if they didn't, couldn't they find a way to learn what they needed to know using less primitive and traumatic methods than abduction, restraint, and experimentation (and certainly without their subject being conscious during the process, thereby negating the need to "wipe" their memories)?

As for the genetic-experiments hypothesis, as we considered earlier this makes even less sense. We've already discussed the impossibility of splicing genetic material from two unrelated species together in an effort to create a "hybrid" alien/human. It would be like trying to combine frog and mouse DNA together in an effort to create a third kind of creature (a furry frog or a mouse with webbed feet perhaps); it simply isn't possible. No matter how physiologically similar an alien species might be to us, there would still be too many dissimilarities in the DNA to make it even theoretically possible to merge the two together in an effort to create a third species. As such, unless we are prepared to rewrite everything we've learned about genetics over the last fifty years, hybrid humans must remain in the realm of fantasy alongside mermaids and half-man/half-horse satyrs.

Modifying human DNA, however, while potentially more feasible (and perhaps logical), forces us to ask the question of why such modifications don't show up in subsequent DNA tests. It seems that were this the case, abductees' DNA should show some evidence of having been tampered with or enhanced in some way, yet to date there is no suggestion that such is the case: as far as can be determined, the genetic makeup of abductees is no different from that of non-abductees, thereby rendering the assumption that aliens are tinkering with our genomes unsupportable by physical evidence.

Finally we come to the problem of abduction memories themselves. It seems that if genetic manipulation or mere physiological studies were the intent of an abduction, an alien race should easily be able to render their subjects unconscious—and, hence, completely oblivious to any procedure (and even the abduction event itself)—thereby negating any potential memories of the event. Yet most abductees report being fully conscious throughout their examinations and even during the abduction event itself, forcing us to ask why.

Some respond to this by maintaining that remaining conscious throughout the abduction experience may be necessary for the procedure to "work," after which time the aliens erase their subject's memories of the event and send them on their way. This is why most people can't consciously recall being abducted except through hypnosis (the "missing time" syndrome); it is because they have had their memories effectively erased by the aliens in an effort to hide their bizarre activity from the authorities (for good reason, one would imagine). Yet here is the problem: if an alien race has the technology to erase a memory (perhaps they have mapped the human brain thoroughly enough to understand how this can be done without damaging the brain itself), then there should *never* be an abduction story because *no such memory any longer resides within the brain*. Yet hundreds of people have come forward to recount remarkably similar stories under hypnosis (and, sometimes, even consciously), demonstrating that if aliens have the ability to remove our memories, they either aren't very good at it or are choosing to simply suppress the memory rather than destroy it for some reason. Why they might want to do this will be discussed in more detail later, but it's important to remember this point.

So in the end we are left with a mystery for both sides to ponder: believers are left with a multitude of sometimes eccentric individuals who have shared an experience that both defies logic and lacks any hard evidence to substantiate their claims, while skeptics are left with a tantalizing trail of life-changing experiences being told by apparently rational and sincere people who seek neither fame (many abductees adamantly refuse to be identified) nor wealth in recounting their experiences. Clearly something is going on, though it remains unclear exactly what that "something" is, how it happens, or why.

Conclusions

What do all these mysteries tell us? It's difficult to imagine that *every* crop circle, *every* cattle mutilation, and *every* account of MIBs and alien abductions are hoaxes, misinterpretations of naturally occurring events, waking dreams, or sheer imagination. Are we truly a species prone to delusion on such a massive scale, or could there be something more going on—something more remarkable than we may have been willing to imagine up to now? Earlier we discussed how we might go about initiating contact with an extraterrestrial race by revealing ourselves incrementally over a long period of time. Is it possible that these mysteries commonly linked to UFOs may be something akin to that—an extraterrestrial effort to get our attention—or even a means of studying how we might respond to certain stimuli? To find the answer, let's reexamine each of these phenomena in the context of an extraterrestrial attempt at making contact to see if we can perceive any common patterns that might help us understand what our friends from the stars might possibly be up to.

chapter fourteen

Exposing the Alien Agenda

In chapter 12, we looked at the possibility that while attempting to make contact with alien species ourselves, as part of stage-two contact it might be necessary for us to suggest our presence without definitively proving it. I noted that such a strategy would be an important means of laying the groundwork for later, direct contact with an advanced but still developing alien civilization. Naturally, then, we can ask ourselves whether or not, if this is what *we* might do, might not an extraterrestrial civilization do the same thing? Could, in fact, these mysteries we've just looked at be evidence that aliens have taken a page from our hypothetical playbook and are using things like crop circles, cattle mutilations, MIBs, and abductions as a part of stage-two contact? In essence, could all these mysteries be taken as evidence that an alien race, or conceivably several of them possibly working in collaboration, is even now busily laying the foundation for later, direct contact?

It would be easy to dismiss such a notion, especially since these mysteries appear to be unrelated; however, I wonder if we are unable to see their linkage because of our tendency to concentrate on each of these phenomena *individually* rather than consider them collectively as pieces of a much larger puzzle that, when joined, form a complete and, some might say, startling picture. To determine whether this is true, let's put these pieces together and see if we can't discern the deeper meaning they may be pointing us toward.

Crop Circles

While it is likely that most crop circles are the work of hoaxers trying to outdo each other, there are some that appear to be genuinely inexplicable to modern science. As such, if we work from the premise that at least a few crop circles may truly be the handiwork of extraterrestrials, we can only ask the question: what are they trying to tell us through them? To answer that, we must step back and look at the phenomenon in its entirety, and when we do, we quickly notice several interesting elements emerge.

Perhaps the single most intriguing aspect of the phenomenon is the significance of where crop circles are most frequently found. From the beginning, circles have been found almost exclusively in wheat or corn fields or, at the very least, in fields where some cash crop is being grown. Rarely are they reported in naturally occurring tall grass, open fields, or in swamps and marshes. So why might this be?

Skeptics would claim that the reason crop circles appear predominantly in fields of cash crops is because of their greater accessibility (crop fields are usually traversed by track lines, allowing for easier access) and because of their pervasive nature (as opposed to grassy fields, which are less common and therefore less accessible). While undoubtedly this would account for why most hoaxed circles are found in crop fields, this doesn't take into account either why they're rarely found outside of them (one would imagine at least some hoaxers would opt for more remote and less problematic sites to display their "art"[43]) or why they often display inexplicable physical anomalies and characteristics. But if extraterrestrials are creating their messages in cash-crop fields, what reason would they have for choosing such a medium beyond those already noted?

Consider what these crops represent. Crops are the agricultural basis of our survival as a species, just as they have been from antiquity, and as such they serve as the perfect metaphor for the advent and growth of human civilization. Could the prevalence of crop circles in these specific locations, then, be a subtle signal that extraterrestrials recognize this fact and place their circles in them specifically to emphasize that point?

Additionally, consider where they are found from a political perspective. While it is assumed that crop circles are a worldwide phenomena, the fact is that they are not; to date, they have appeared in only about thirty countries (out of nearly two hundred on the planet) and almost always in technologically advanced nations such as the United States, Canada, Australia, and the countries of western Europe (particularly the United Kingdom). While a few have been reported in poorer, third world countries, for the most part they appear to "cluster" in very specific countries, countries that are considered to be the most militarily and politically powerful on the planet. Why is this?

Skeptics point to two facts to account for this trend: first, they note that these countries are major grain-producing nations, thereby providing more "canvases" for copycat hoaxers to paint upon and, second, since they assume the entire phenomenon is nothing more than a bizarre competition between practical jokesters, it simply suggests that more affluent cultures have more leisure time—and

---

43. One argument is that circles are more likely to be noticed when they appear in a field of wheat or corn as opposed to an open meadow, where the hoaxers' "art" might well lie undetected and, as such, unappreciated. However, this objection still doesn't account for the physical anomalies often seen in "true" circles, suggesting that even if hoaxers are using wheat fields due to their accessibility and advertisement value, "something else" is also using them as well, though probably not for the same reasons.

perhaps proclivity—toward such silliness than do less affluent cultures.

While both objections need to be considered, I still wonder if it's as simple as that. It *appears* as though crop circles are being deliberately and consistently produced predominately where they are most likely to be found, reported, and studied. Does this not suggest that the phenomenon may be carefully targeted toward a particular audience (and one that seems to be slowly growing over time as more countries report the strange circles of crushed crops)? Consider that crop circles have most recently been reported in China and India, along with a few other Asian-rim countries. Is it just a coincidence that these countries are just starting to emerge on the world stage as industrial and political powers and, as such, the next best target audiences on our rapidly industrializing planet?

But why would extraterrestrials do this—if, indeed, they are the force responsible for at least a few of these circles? Only one explanation makes sense, especially if we consider the issue from the perspective of an extraterrestrial visitor: extraterrestrials are using crop circles as a means of communication—calling cards of their presence, so to speak—designed to send us subtle evidence of their presence and gauge our ability to unlock their codes. As a communication tool, crop circles are perfect: sophisticated enough to convince some they are of extraterrestrial origin but not so sophisticated that they are capable of convincing a hardened skeptic. As such, those who want to understand the messages "get them," while those who do not can dismiss the entire phenomenon as so much nonsense. A more perfect camouflage could not be found.

However, even more than a tool for communication, could they also be using them as a mechanism by which to study human behavior on a grand scale—more specifically how we respond to unexplained and mysterious phenomena in our midst? If so, I'd imagine crop circles and the controversy surrounding them could tell our extraterrestrial observers much about human nature: for example, it might appear curious to them that some people would embrace the entire phenomenon so completely that they would create a proto-science designed specifically to study it, and even more remarkable that we would spend so much time and energy attempting to prove, disprove, and even replicate the phenomenon. If nothing else, it would clearly demonstrate to our visitors the human fascination for anything unknown and mysterious, as well as our propensity for trying to mimic such phenomena. This knowledge would provide them an insight into the human psyche that nothing else in the human experience could do and give them a much better understanding of how we think. Even if extraterrestrials are responsible for only a tiny percentage of crop circles, our response to the entire phenomenon itself—including the proclivity toward hoaxing the phenomenon on a massive scale—might be quite educational to an extraterrestrial observer.

Cattle Mutilations

Even if we can accept that crop circles are an essentially harmless means that extraterrestrials might use to make themselves known to us, how could cattle mutilations (which, interestingly, began to be noticed around the same time as crop circles first began to come on the scene) perform the same function? Whereas crop circles elicit wonder and reverence and even a sense of fun, cattle mutilations elicit only fear and foreboding and often a feeling of paranoia. Would extraterrestrials really use such a brutal tactic to communicate with us, and if they are, what is their message?

It's important to consider that cattle and other farm animals, like the grain fields crop circles are usually found in, also represent an important aspect of humanity's means of survival. Meat is a staple of our diet and has been instrumental in our rise as a civilization. Could mutilations, then, simply represent the fact that "they" appreciate and, perhaps, even control this element of our continual survival as well? Agriculture and ranching = crop circles and dead cattle. An intriguing thought.

Mutilations also demonstrate something more: that extraterrestrials possess the technology to seize animals from our pastures without our noticing them and return them, again without our awareness, wherever and, apparently, whenever they wish. Like crop circles, then, cattle mutilations are also a means of studying us, perhaps by touching upon our fears more than our sense of wonder (as is the case with the more benign crop circles). After all, were extraterrestrials intent on contacting us they would need to understand how the mechanism of fear operates in human beings and how that fear might manifest itself if contact were made. It would also be important for an alien civilization to gauge how we respond to perceived threats on a personal and emotional level, which would constitute a very important type of knowledge they could acquire only by incorporating such unorthodox and, some might say, controversial tactics. Is this why mutilated animals are left where they can be easily found and eviscerated in such a way as to appear the victims of an alien and exotic—and potentially lethal—technology? Cattle mutilations, then, while appearing cruel from our perspective, could actually be an important learning tool for our alien visitors as they watch how we react to these seemingly random—but actually carefully planned—acts of apparent barbarism.

Finally, it would be an opportunity to see if humans would mimic the mutilation process in the same way they do crop circles, thereby telling the visitors even more about ourselves. It's important to note that as far as can be determined, no one has ever been caught attempting to duplicate a cattle mutilation. One hopes this is perceived by extraterrestrials as a positive sign.

However, doesn't this hypothesis imply a malevolent element to extraterrestrials? Does it not, in fact, suggest that they may be what some have accused them of being from the beginning: cold, disinterested observers with no more compassion for us than we might have toward a colony of ants? To that extent, might it not even imply that they could be "evil"—as we would define the term—and capable of great destruction if they so choose?

It could, but I suspect that would be reading too much into the phenomenon. That we would accuse extraterrestrials of being evil because they mutilate cattle is to demonstrate a remarkable inconsistency in our sense of moral outrage; after all, we slaughter many thousands of cattle each day in our quest for nourishment, yet find the mutilation of a comparative handful of animals over a period of decades somehow morally reprehensible. Are cattle mutilations, then, another means of telling the extraterrestrials—and perhaps ourselves—something about our moral nature and sense of ethics? It's an interesting question.

MIBs (Men in Black)

If extraterrestrials want to understand us in all our many guises, they will need to know not only how we would respond to external mysteries but how we would react to internal or personal mysteries as well. Perhaps the best way to test this aspect of our psyches is by observing how we humans interact with those fellow humans we perceive to be mysterious or peculiar. As such, whereas crop circles and cattle mutilations are means of gauging mankind's reaction to effects on his physical environment, could the quirky little Men in Black (MIBs)—people perfectly designed to test the limits of human interaction and intimidation—be their way of studying our sociological responses?

However, if part of some elaborate extraterrestrial sociological study, that doesn't explain whether these beings are aliens disguised as humans or, as I suggested earlier, androids of some type (or even, perhaps, human agents under extraterrestrial control or, at least, employment). Unfortunately, none of these possibilities would explain how they can seemingly appear or disappear so suddenly (and if humans under extraterrestrial employment, why none has ever stepped forward to confess), leaving each of these possibilities untenable. As such, perhaps we need to stretch our imagination a bit to find the answer and approach the question from the perspective of an ultra-advanced alien civilization in possession of a level of technology we can only equate with magic.

Imagine, then, that MIBs are not humans, aliens, or androids— neither organic nor mechanical in nature—but are instead holographs? Wouldn't that explain how they can suddenly appear and disappear with such ease and why they seem "almost" human but not quite so?[44] Additionally, holographic projections would solve a number of problems inherent to interacting with alien species: it would eliminate the possibility of cross-contamination, allow the extraterrestrials to alter their projections to fit any venue, and even make it possible to produce silent, black helicopters (something that is clearly impossible to do in an atmosphere). As such, might not MIBs be but illusions designed to give our visitors an opportunity to interact with us in a way they could not do otherwise?

Yet that doesn't entirely explain *why* MIBs act in the often unusual ways that they do. They seem awkward and ill at ease by most accounts, as though they are *trying* to be a little unusual. Could this be evidence of an alien sense of humor, an imperfect effort at mimicry, or could it be an intentional anomaly designed to add one more layer of intrigue for them to study? After all, they can learn most of what they need to know about human interactions by simply observing us on a daily basis, but watching us respond to people who are clearly unusual or eccentric might be more difficult to observe.

But what of the vague threats witnesses to MIBs sometimes report? Again, is this just another observation of what humans do when they feel intimidated and therefore another invaluable bit of useful knowledge to acquire before contemplating direct contact? I'd imagine that, if done correctly, an MIB encounter could teach

---

44. MIBs, however, have been observed to interact with objects (e.g., hold a glass of water, handle photographs, and so on), thereby challenging the holographic premise. However, could these projections be more than purely visual projections, but contain force fields within them that make them capable of doing things like handling solid objects and leaving footprints in the snow?

an observer much about human nature, thereby further setting the stage for later genuine interaction between species.

Alien Abductions

Finally there is the issue of alien abductions to consider and how they might fit in with my theory. After all, if crop circles and cattle mutilations are designed to test our reactions to external stimuli and MIBs a means of determining how we might respond to unexpected and quirky personal stimuli, how would abductions fit into the mix? If they're not for the purpose of medical research or genetic manipulation (both concepts that we explored earlier), then what might be the rationale behind these often bizarre and traumatizing experiences that so many thousands of people worldwide have claimed to experience?

Consider how, if an alien civilization wanted to explore the most primordial levels of the human psyche, the abduction phenomenon might prove a most useful technique for doing so. After all, perhaps the most basic human fear, besides the fear of death, is the fear of being incarcerated against one's will and sexually violated, both of which are frequently the central theme in many abductions. Is the prospect of being forcefully abducted by strange creatures and experimented upon the means by which they can observe the most primal fears that reside deep within us, thereby revealing much about human nature?

However, what about the earlier objection that abductions are almost never witnessed by third parties, thereby suggesting that they are not literal events but mere delusions? Doesn't this seem to argue against the possibility that they are being performed as a type of psychological study?

Not necessarily. For an alien to understand how we would react in the face of perceived danger, it is not only unnecessary to physically abduct their subjects, but it may be far easier and safer to abduct *only their minds*. In effect, I submit that in the case of alien abductions, aliens aren't *literally* abducting human beings from their cars and bedrooms and dragging them off to some laboratory somewhere to see how they respond to such a violation of their personal will, but are producing their effects entirely *through the subtle manipulations of the human brain itself.*

It's a well documented fact that the brain can be stimulated to produce any number of emotional effects—from euphoria and the sense of floating on air to paranoia and abject terror—simply by touching different areas of the cerebral cortex with a small electrical probe. In fact, researchers have discovered they are capable of mimicking many of the experiences NDE (Near Death Experience) patients often report (i.e., seeing bright lights, a tunnel effect, meeting deceased family or religious figures, and so on) simply by stimulating different areas of the brain with a series of electrically charged magnets. If we can produce such effects in a laboratory with relative ease, then, isn't it possible that extraterrestrials, perhaps after years of mapping the human brain, have acquired the same ability to produce artificially induced hallucinations, making it possible to observe their subject's reactions without even necessitating that the victim leave the comfort of their bed? From the victim's perspective, of course, the abduction would "feel" quite real, allowing them to remain steadfast in their story (enough so to easily pass a polygraph exam) and utterly honest in their reactions.

This would answer several questions regarding the abduction phenomenon: the inexplicable loss of time, the lack of witnesses to an abduction, the similarity of the abductors in most accounts, the apparent realism of the encounter, and so forth, as well as again solving the problem of cross-contamination. In fact, this might even explain some of the earliest contactee reports from the 1950s, in which seemingly sane men and women made the most outrageous claims of having been approached by aliens and given rides to Venus and Jupiter. Undoubtedly some of these individuals were hoaxers or outright delusional, although it seems presumptuous to label all of them as such. Obviously, if aliens possess the technology to stimulate our brains into imagining any number of things, they have possessed this ability for some time and may have used it in years past as well as continuing to refine it today as an important tool in their research.[45]

There is at least one documented incident that appears to sup-port this hypothesis. British UFO investigator and author Nick Pope writes about a 1973 case in which an Australian woman by the name of Maureen Puddy recounted having been abducted by aliens and taken into their vessel while sitting in her car. The only problem was that, at least according to two Australian UFO inves-tigators, Paul Norman and Judith Magee, who were sitting next to her throughout the experience, *she never left her car.* According to Pope:

> . . . *while in the company of Norman and Magee, she [Mrs. Puddy] shouted out that she could see the alien, and there then followed an extraordinary narrative in which she described how she had been kidnapped, and was now inside the UFO. At all times during the narrative she was sitting in the seat of her car, in full sight of the UFO investigators, and at one stage she seemed to be in a trance-like state.*[46]

Pope goes on to ask whether this could have been evidence of fraud or delusion before finally asking if it might not have been ". . . a real event that took place in a different reality, which Maureen Puddy could somehow glimpse, while Norman and Magee could not?"

Could this be closer to the truth than many might imagine? For that matter, could Mrs. Puddy's experience, rather than being

---

45. For that matter, could the infamous "grays" of abduction legend then be creations of these extraterrestrials designed to facilitate the process? In other words, could they be constructs designed for our benefit based upon what extraterrestrials have determined through lengthy studies of our culture and mythology to be our archetypes of what we imagine aliens "should" look like? That would go far in explaining not only the consistency of descriptions given in most abduction accounts but their evolution from Nordic-looking figures of the 1950s to the more insect-like or reptilian ETs commonly seen today.

46. Nick Pope, *The Uninvited: An Exposé of the Alien Abduction Phenomenon.* New York: Pocket Books, 1998, 54.

an anomaly, be instead the *norm* for abduction experiences? The only difference between her experience and that of nearly all other abductees is that hers was witnessed whereas most abductions are not. As such, is it possible that most—possibly even *all* abductees— are only experiencing the abduction event *in their minds* and not in their physical reality at all, apparently as Maureen Puddy did? If such truly were the case, it would solve many of the difficulties the abduction phenomenon presents (lack of witnesses, multiple abductees, the marked absence of physical evidence of an abduction, and so forth) while remaining a real event and, potentially, evidence of genuine alien communication (or, more precisely, experimentation).

Of course, an induced hallucination is not necessarily the only possibility. I suggested a moment ago that MIBs may in fact be holographic projections designed to study our interactions with those we consider intimidating or odd. Could "grays," then, along with their instruments and examining room, also be holographic in nature?

It's possible but I think unlikely. Abductees have reported being touched and handled by their captors and of having seemingly very solid metallic instruments inserted into their bodies, all of which would be difficult to do with a hologram (additionally, there would still be the problem with detection. Even holographic abductors would be seen by witnesses as they spirited away a terrified human.) If there is any validity to the alien abduction phenomenon at all, it could only be if it takes place in the mind as a carefully implanted memory created by a cunning and sophisticated race.

But what then of these suppressed memories? If an alien race has the ability to imprint such vivid hallucinations into the human brain, why do they seemingly lack the ability to remove those memories—and the resultant trauma—once they've finished? Why let people go on suffering fear and anxiety for years afterward when it would seem to be such a simple thing to spare them such trauma? The fact that they don't take this basic step suggests that *they wish* to induce these memories, likely in an effort to study the trauma itself. In effect, aliens don't want to just understand how we would react to an abduction experience at the moment it happens, but how we respond to it days, weeks, even years later (as well as observe how others respond to their accounts as well). This is a study that may be happening on a number of levels, each part of which is equally important toward creating an overall and complete understanding of the human psyche.

But this still leaves us to ponder the question of whether this doesn't make our observers monsters for inducing this effect in people. After all, they still leave their victims traumatized and frightened, so what does it matter if the abduction takes place *only* in the mind; rape is still rape whether it be of the body *or* of the mind.

Perhaps, but I suspect that from their perspective, the varying degrees of trauma may be seen merely as the unfortunate byproduct of a necessary process, all of it ultimately designed for our own good. Just as a needle causes short-term pain but ultimately brings relief from long-term disease, so too may the psychological experiments they carry out on us eventually bring relief from ignorance and our isolation in the cosmos. We are being prepped, I believe, prepared for an uncertain but exciting future among the stars, and alien abductions may merely be one small part of the process that will take us there. Consider that we daily inject horses with live snake venom so that they will produce the necessary antitoxins in their blood to fight the poison—which we then remove from the animal and use to save hundreds of lives every year. Would the horses consider us cruel for doing this if they knew what we were injecting into their bodies, or would they consider us saints once they understood why we were doing it? The answer is always simple when one considers only a single point of view.

Conclusions

So, where is this all taking us? Are we ready for contact or do we require more time before we are prepared to meet our cosmic brethren face to face? My guess is that considering the present state of affairs—our deep fear of each other and the future, our unpredictability and paranoia, and our growing distrust for the institutions that keep us organized and stable—we're not yet ready to take that step. One day in the hopefully not-too-distant future we will be ready, but until then we will simply have to endure more of the process. "They" still have much to learn about us before they can begin to understand the mechanism by which we humans operate and before they are ready to make contact. If our cosmic colleagues gave themselves away now, they would not only create a panic among their subjects, but, worse, they would lose the opportunity to watch our burgeoning civilization find the strength to repair itself and move beyond its fear-based mentality. I suspect there are more than a few of these beings pulling for us to drag ourselves from the morass of thousands of years of war, oppression, hatred, and fear and make our way to the stars to join them, which will, in the end, not only make sense of this whole experience we call life but make it a worthwhile journey to take.

chapter fifteen

Facing an Uncertain Future

What conclusions might we come to with regard to this whole process and, even more importantly, how might we use these conclusions to make some predictions about the future and the possibilities for eventual contact? Attempting to answer such questions may well be a fool's game, but being that this entire book is an exercise in "what ifs," I am prepared to go where angels fear to tread and make a few predictions. While admittedly these are only my opinions, I believe them to be both credible and self-evident once we carefully consider each of them in turn for a moment.

First, it appears to me to be not only possible but probable that extraterrestrials are observing our planet and have been for some time. There are simply too many real-life experiences from reliable witnesses to dismiss everything as a media-driven fantasy, hoaxes, and misidentifications of the planet Venus. Obviously, much of the evidence is tainted or otherwise questionable, and some of the witnesses uncertain or simply mistaken, but there remains a core of evidence that is difficult to explain away, even with all the deductive skills at our disposal. In fact, if there is advanced life in the universe at all—

life that is capable of interstellar flight on any level—then extraterrestrial visitation is not only probable, but even to be expected. This is not a statement purely of faith—though there is an element of that—but of statistical and scientific probability. It is the chances *against* there being extraterrestrials that, in my opinion, are the longer odds.

Second, I believe there is more than one race observing us, which explains the often bewildering array of different craft and alien "types" that have been reported over the decades. I imagine our planet to be a major point of interest in this area of space, not because we harbor life (many planets can probably make that claim) but because we are getting "interesting" to other races, especially since the start of the atomic age. Before that we were probably merely an anthropological curiosity, but now that we are on the verge of joining them among the stars, they are starting to take notice of us, which is what I believe explains the burgeoning of UFO reports since the end of World War II.

Third, I believe extraterrestrials have been observing us for thousands and potentially even millions of years, as implied by the scattering of clues they have left throughout our mythology. I do not believe, however, that they established civilization, built our pyramids, showed us how to create fire, or gave us blueprints to the wheel. Observed us, yes, but interacted with us in significant ways—at least intentionally—no. Whether these are the same races that are observing us now is unknown—I suspect that such races come and go, making the current "crop" likely unique to human history—but one never knows; there may well be ancient races out there that measure their decades and centuries the way we measure days and weeks, making them ancient intellects that possess a degree of patience we can only imagine.

Fourth, I do not believe these visitors—at least the majority of them—to be malevolent or that they intend us harm. Were they either, they would have moved against us long ago—especially when we were in less of a position to resist. While they may not necessarily be beings of light and love, anxious to show us the way to creating our own utopian planet, I suspect they are probably far more spiritually advanced than ourselves in many ways and, as such, generally benevolent (and, perhaps, even maternal in some ways). At a minimum, I imagine them to be indifferent observers intent on studying us in much the same way we would study the tribespeople of New Guinea (except that they are capable of doing so without the temptation to "civilize" us as we so frequently feel compelled to do to others). However, I also suspect that at least some of them are master manipulators, capable of playing games with our minds in an effort to determine what really makes us tick. Some might consider this evidence of a cold and calloused intellect—or even of great evil if one were so inclined—but that would be purely the perspective the mouse might hold toward the scientist who keeps making it run through a maze. They may actually possess genuine affection for us—much as the scientist might have toward his mice—but that doesn't stop them from finding out what they need to know. They aren't playing games but acquiring knowledge—knowledge that not only will prove beneficial to them but ultimately will be used to our benefit as well—someday, when we are ready.

Future Possibilities

But what of the future? If my hypothesis that extraterrestrials are taking us through a process designed to ultimately lead us into first contact is correct, what might we expect them to do next? Obviously, any guesses would be pure speculation, but I am willing to offer them if only in keeping with the spirit of this tome.

First, I would expect to see crop circles turn up in more countries and become even more prevalent in nations that are on the verge of achieving superpower status, such as India, China, and Brazil. As of this writing, crop circles have only been found in about thirty countries—almost all of them in Europe. In the next few decades, however, expect to find them appearing with greater frequency and complexity around the world, not as hoaxers get in on the fun in ever-increasing numbers (though that will be an element of it) but as our extraterrestrial friends gradually expand their efforts. Also look for their messages to take on ever more complexity and sophistication as we get better at playing their game (i.e., the mouse gets better at running the maze), forcing them to build better mazes for us to run through.

I suspect that cattle mutilations will also continue, but I look for them to begin turning up in the lesser-developed countries of the world where the phenomena has not been as well-publicized, all designed to carefully gauge the unique reactions each culture would offer to these grisly but essentially harmless experiments (at least, harmless to humans). I believe extraterrestrials are trying to understand the concept of superstition and the role it plays in the human psyche, and so may find it helpful to expand their experiments beyond the narrow range of countries seen up to now and into areas that have had no previous experience with such phenomena.

I have no idea what to say about MIBs and alien abductions, however. My guess is that such reports will continue (especially abductions) but, being that they are rapidly losing their novelty, they may begin to lose their impact as a study subject (at least, inside those cultures that have had considerable experience with the phenomenon). However, I wouldn't be surprised to see extraterrestrials shift their tactics from abductions to introducing subconsciously induced contact instead, perhaps through the use of channeling and other more traditionally paranormal methodology. I should think this would be a valuable area of study to them, as well as an even more effective way of revealing their presence to us.

Another good possibility is that extraterrestrials are on the verge of "ratcheting up" their appearances and allowing themselves to be seen and filmed by ever larger numbers of people, hopefully encouraging the normally cynical media to start taking the subject more seriously. As such, I wouldn't be surprised if over the next few years several very well-documented appearances—with clear camera footage and hundreds of reliable eyewitnesses—occur around the world, many of them compelling enough to make even the scientific community take notice. On a related note, I'd also look for the governments of the world to become more forthcoming with what they know about UFOs in the next few years in an effort to rebuild the trust of the citizenry by declassifying much—though not all—of what they know. This is only a guess, of course, but if the government (ours or anyone else's) does have information on this subject they have been suppressing over the years, it would be to their advantage to tell what they know—within reason—if they want to make themselves a key player in the eventual first-contact game.

But does all this mean we may be on the verge of first contact, then? Are these occurrences to be interpreted as signs that our isolation in the universe may be coming to an end? It's hard to say. We don't know how far along our observers are in the process; they may still be in the earliest stages and are just beginning to increase the frequency and potency of each event to gauge our responses, or they may be in the final stages and on the verge of moving on to stage-three contact. My guess, however, is that even if they are concluding their initial studies, they may be in no particular hurry to contact us. They may even have other mysteries they intend to spring on us first, or perhaps they are content to simply wait until we reach a technological level at which space travel is increasingly feasible for our species before they take the next step. In any case, it appears likely that we are being "prepped" for something in much the same way a Marine recruit is prepared for combat. Hopefully, however, we are not being prepared to fight our guests but join with them in a mutually beneficial dialogue that will set us on the path toward our own future among the stars.

As part of that preparation, I might make one more prediction, though I suspect it to be one that may not be realized in my lifetime. As we embark on missions to the moon and Mars over the next few decades, look for two things to happen that will dramatically change the way we look at our place in the cosmos: first, expect scientists to definitively discover evidence of microbial life on the red planet—either past or present—thereby demonstrating life to be ubiquitous in the universe, and second, look for extraterrestrials to leave some sort of "calling card" for us to discover on one of these planets, thereby setting the stage for eventual contact. It won't be anything as extravagant as abandoned domed cities or a dust-covered spaceport, but more likely something small and innocuous such as a simple artifact of obvious extraterrestrial manufacture. It will be quite a sensation, of course, but it would be imperative in helping humanity mentally prepare itself for the prospect of first contact (and perhaps usher in a new golden age of space exploration in the process).

Conclusions

All of these predictions may prove erroneous, of course, but I believe that first contact—whatever form it takes—to be inevitable. Whether we will be prepared to take advantage of the tremendous opportunity that event will afford us remains to be seen, but I suspect that extraterrestrials don't waste their time and resources attempting to communicate with "lost causes." It's even possible they have a more optimistic assessment of us than we hold for ourselves and are eagerly awaiting the opportunity to tell us all about themselves once we have matured to the point that we will be able to hear them. Until then, however, we will just have to be patient and know that our opportunity to take our place in the cosmos is only a matter of time.

Someday we will be someone else's extraterrestrials—another race's UFOs and curious phenomenon—and that's when we will know we have arrived. And when we do, we will have earned the right to be there—a right due all sentient beings wherever they may be who have managed to overcome countless centuries of turmoil and strife in their quest to take their rightful place among the stars.

Humanity faces a bright future if only we can suppress our fear of that future and embrace it as the gift it is, and only time will tell if—and when—we will be ready when the opportunity to seize that golden age is presented to us.

An Alien Perspective on Earth

Before finishing, I thought it might be fun to take a moment and imagine how we might appear to an extraterrestrial race that has been observing us for some time. As such, I've put together this little tongue-in-cheek status report—sent by an alien observer to his superior—for you to consider. Hopefully, in seeing the situation from their viewpoint, it'll provide an insight into the whole affair that's difficult to appreciate from our limited perspective. Obviously, it's not meant to be taken seriously and I hope the reader will take it in the spirit in which it's intended.

STATUS REPORT: 1015-A
SUBJECT PLANET: AX-65447 (Colloquially known as "Earth")
NATURE OF REPORT: Evaluation of human subjects and their reactions to our first contact efforts
COMMENCE TRANSMISSION: In keeping with your request, Prefect, that I provide you with my impressions of our study subjects, I submit this report—the first of what I anticipate to be many—for you to consider. I apologize that it has taken three full

cycles to complete these observations, but these beings are so fascinating that it has been difficult to pull myself away long enough to record my thoughts—just as you said they would be.

First, your original assessment of them—corroborated by several other races that have also observed them in the past—is proving increasingly accurate. They are, indeed, a species that thrives on inconsistencies, some of which I note here:

1. They are an extremely fearful species seemingly bent on both their own destruction while at the same time demonstrating a determination to survive at all costs, making them both unpredictable and mildly dangerous at the same time. They are the only life form I am aware of that will knowingly create the means to destroy itself and then forfeit its own long-term safety by knowingly selling that technology to the highest bidder for short-term gain, again demonstrating their primitive shortsightedness. I suspect it is only a matter of time before this gap in their logic will result in considerable destruction, forcing them to reevaluate this self-destructive tendency within themselves.

2. Speaking of short-term gain at the expense of long-term security, they continue to squander their natural resources at an alarming rate as well as ravage their environment in their ongoing and never-ending accumulation of wealth and comfort. For some reason they appear intent on deforesting their planet, despite the fact that it is their forests that produce the bulk of their oxygen supply, and are willing to pollute their atmosphere in the quest for more energy, with which they use to create usually unnecessary material goods of dubious value or fuel their thirst for entertainment. (There even seems to be a city in what's known as the American southwest designed almost exclusively for entertainment and the acquisition of wealth, requiring vast amounts of energy and resources to maintain its workforce and clientele. Are you aware of any similar examples

of this elsewhere in the galactic arm? I have been unable to locate any in my searches of the anthropological records.)

3. They appear to be very materialistic creatures, many of whom spend much of their lives in the pursuit of more luxurious dwellings, larger personal transportation vehicles, and recreational items of all kinds. What I find especially curious about this is that they don't seem to be satisfied with whatever level of procurement they are at, and are always looking to "upgrade" to larger and more expensive possessions. Some will even spend far more time at their vocations than is reasonable in an effort to earn sufficient monetary resources to maintain this pursuit, sometimes even at the cost of their own health and family cohesion.

4. I have noticed that they appear to be terrified of the biological process, especially the termination of it (that which they call "death"), and are willing to go to great lengths to avoid it—sometimes even to the point of causing the termination of their fellow humans in the quest to survive. Yet at the same time, they engage in all manner of unhealthy and dangerous lifestyles and pursuits, and then feel that life is "unfair" if they should fall victim to them. They even produce substances, both legally and illegally, that can be ingested, inhaled, and otherwise introduced into their bodies and are proven to have a deleterious—and, in many cases, even lethal—effect on them, yet they continue to insist on their "right" to manufacture, purchase, and use these dangerous items.

5. They seem to excel at hyperbole, exaggeration, and deception while attempting to maintain the illusion that they remain "open-minded" about a host of subjects they have long since decided on. It is truly fascinating how they will believe almost anything as long as it conforms to their preconceived biases while rejecting—sometimes violently—anything that challenges their beliefs, be they religious, scientific, political, or

philosophical in nature. It is curious that despite the tremendous advances in science, mathematics, and even philosophy humans have made over the last thirty cycles (that which they call a "century"), they remain remarkably resistant to new ideas and often will attack them outright. I suspect this is because they find comfort in the familiar and traditional while perceiving the new and different as a threat to their security. Still, I find it remarkable that a society that has come so far should still be so resistant to anything they don't immediately understand.

6. They have a curious tendency to place each other into various subgroups, which is, I believe, their way of maintaining control and order. These subgroups, however, are not as much organized along purely racial, religious, and gender lines as are most primitive cultures (and as they once were) but are increasingly being determined by economic, political, and professional considerations. In other words, it appears that one's place in this order is dependent upon how much education and opportunity they have achieved rather than mere birthright, as has traditionally been the case. Economic status, then, appears to supersede the traditional divisions, though only to a degree; even within the highest levels of their social strata, racial, religious, and gender differences remain, though they are less apparent than in earlier times.

7. They are a superstitious and religious people, willing to fight to the death for their beliefs—even at the point of self-destruction. I have observed the most remarkable behavior in this regard, with both males and females of the species demonstrating the willingness to destroy their own and their progeny's futures for the sake of being in obedience to whatever tribal or cultural deities they profess allegiance to. They seem entirely unaware or indifferent to the fact that they are all of the same race, preferring instead to see each other—even those who pose no immediate threat to themselves—as a pestilence in need of extermination. I am truly amazed the planet has not

torn itself to pieces over these often trivial differences long ago, but then I understand that such factional differences are common among the more primitive races. Still, the viciousness and ruthlessness with which some practice their "faith" still catches me by surprise.

But I have also noticed some positive signs as well—ones that I failed to see noted in your earlier reports to me. (I'm not certain if that was intentional on your part or merely an oversight, but I suspect the latter.) However, to make this report as complete as possible, I note the following evidence of progress among our subjects as well:

1. Although a primitive race prone toward violence and self-absorption, they are also a race capable of great compassion and the potential of realizing considerable spiritual growth. I have noticed, in fact, that most of this race will, under certain circumstances, consistently demonstrate mercy and forgiveness even against many of their most implacable adversaries. This is in sharp contrast to most of the primitives I have observed, who consider the extermination of their competitors their main objective; these humans, in contrast, appear to abhor the concept of totally annihilating their adversaries and have even been known to utilize considerable amounts of their own resources in an effort to assist in their vanquished foe's recovery and rebuilding efforts. I perceive this to be a major strength within them.

2. While still suspicious of others, they are slowly learning to accept and, in some cases, even embrace their differences, making them collectively stronger in the process. This is a huge advance over thirty cycles ago when they rejected anything and anyone different from themselves and suppressed, exterminated, enslaved, or marginalized those they considered "inferior" for their own assumed self-importance. The one example that comes to mind is that of slavery, which had been

a major element of the race's economic vitality for many cycles but has long since been outlawed (if not entirely eliminated) throughout the planet. As you know, this has always been an important benchmark in assessing the spiritual progress of any primitive race and, as such, appears to speak favorably of humans in general.

3. While warlike, most of them appear to desire a change from that method of solving their disputes. A good example of this can be seen on the continent they call Europe; once the source of many of the planet's largest and most destructive conflicts, today it appears to be in the process of unifying itself under a common economic, military, and political banner, greatly reducing the likelihood of armed conflict occurring among the more than forty countries that occupy the continent. While there still remain a handful of nations on the planet dedicated to the use of force to solve differences, they are becoming increasingly uncommon and marginalized, making it possible, should armed conflicts erupt—as they still occasionally do—to keep them generally small and contained. Further, the prospects of large conflicts between what they call the "superpowers" has diminished greatly since the end of the dangerous period in their history known as the "Cold War." While their nuclear arsenals remain extensive, the chances of them using them against each other appears to be greatly diminished though not, as I'm sure you're aware, entirely eliminated. I suspect this demonstrates that they are capable of learning from their past mistakes and are becoming increasingly cognizant of the ever-greater cost armed conflict demands of them—costs they are becoming increasingly unwilling to bear.

4. I am also pleased to note the dramatic shift from totalitarian and authoritarian regimes to those that provide greater levels of self-determination—especially in the last thirty cycles. Consider that when our earliest probes first mapped the planet, that which they call "democratic" governments were in the

minority; today, in contrast, those regimes not democratic in nature constitute the minority—again, another important benchmark in bringing this race in line with current accepted minimal levels of progress. At their current rate of political evolution, I foresee an entirely self-determining political infrastructure fully in place by the end of their next "century."

5. Traditionally unconcerned with the health of their planet, I perceive a significant shift in this perception as well, even within the largest and most industrialized nations. Emissions standards are being significantly improved and a genuine effort at shifting from a petroleum and coal-based economy toward clean and renewable energy sources is growing in momentum. While economic considerations are sometimes retarding this progression, even the planet's industrialists are beginning to see the wisdom of changing direction, while the world governments are also beginning to appreciate the political advantage in tapping inexhaustible and renewable sources of energy rather than making themselves increasingly dependent upon foreign and, sometimes, unreliable energy sources. Our scientists expect to see this trend increase, especially as concerns over global warming consume more of their attention and elicit increased demands for change as their technological ability to take advantage of renewable energy sources becomes increasingly developed.

6. Though they are still intransigent in terms of their religious and philosophical beliefs, I do see progress in their willingness to be more accommodating and tolerant of different approaches to spirituality, at least in some regions, and therefore less prone toward using violence to preserve their cherished and traditional belief structures. This is not true everywhere, of course, but it is a positive trend I have been noting for some time, and one that seems to be on the rise. Could it be evidence that they are making progress spiritually, or is it merely an anomaly that will disappear the moment they feel threatened? Only time will tell.

Considering all these factors, then, and while it remains to be seen if they may not yet make a fatal miscalculation, I personally remain optimistic about the eventual prospect of contacting this race. I do agree, however, that they are not yet ready to accept us, for they still have much fear and superstition to overcome before that day can be realized. As such, I recommend that we continue with our acclimation efforts until they are more amenable to our presence.

In an earlier transmission you asked for my appraisal of the various methods currently being employed in this regard, which I am only too happy to provide. It is no secret that I personally find our use of electromagnetic configuration techniques—that which they call "crop circles"—to be the most effective means of preparing this race for eventual contact, and of course I remain an enthusiastic proponent not only of its continued use but of expanding its role. We have made considerable inroads with this procedure, even to the point that some of their own scientists are beginning to consider the "crop circles" as potentially significant.

I suppose my biggest surprise to date, though, has not been their inability to entirely understand the geometric and mathematical equations encoded within them, but their curious tendency to mimic them by attempting to create their own crude circles. This is not done in an apparent effort to learn how we create them, but in an effort to deceive each other, suggesting that they apparently find the prospect of "tricking" each other more satisfying than attempting to learn the truth about the circles. I also find curious the vehemence with which those who are unable to accept the possibility that we are responsible for many of the circles and attack those who are more amenable to the idea. Do you imagine that is a result of fear, or simply evidence of an obstinate unwillingness to consider other possibilities?

I am less certain about the value of continuing to leave evidence of our technological capabilities on the carcasses of their livestock, however. That aspect of the experiment, while interesting, appears to be less beneficial and only seems to enhance their already deep-seated paranoia. I know these decisions are not mine to make and there are those within the collective who want to continue and even expand these efforts, but I personally find them less than useful—especially when compared to the more benign and less intimidating (to them) crop circles—and even potentially counter-productive. We already have a fairly comprehensive understanding of how they respond to these experiments, so I am unable to perceive what benefit there would be in continuing them.

The MIB and abduction experiments are more useful in understanding the human psyche, I admit, but, again, I think that at least as far as the abduction experiments go, our entire methodology may need to be reconsidered. I am growing increasingly convinced that these procedures may be doing more harm than good, even if that harm is not physical in nature—mental and emotional anguish being every bit as traumatic—and should be discontinued. Of course, I understand the purpose behind them and agree that the data they provide is priceless, but I still can't believe that purposely traumatizing our subjects through this process is a particularly moral or scientifically useful way of learning what we need to know.

Finally, Prefect, my recommendations for the future—beyond those I have already stated—is that we should consider making ourselves even more obvious to the humans by allowing ourselves to be more clearly and frequently recorded on their visual and electronic devices, and perhaps even consider broadcasting some subtle but obvious signals of our presence to their radio detection equipment. I know these are controversial steps and may be considered premature, but it is my opinion that such methods may be a means of forcing our subjects to look beyond their own concerns and consider their place within a much larger universe, thereby perhaps bringing some degree of stability to their chaotic world. I know we are working from a carefully constructed timetable and recognize that impatience is not conducive to useful scientific observation, but I believe our subjects may be getting close to accepting our presence without the fear and panic our superiors presume to be inevitable were we to make contact before completing the assimilation process. That is just an opinion, of course, but one based on many cycles of observing these races. I only hope we may initiate contact before they do themselves in, for they appear to be a noble race worthy of further study.

Warmest Regards,

Treon,

First Overseer, Third Psychological Unit

TERMINATE TRANSMISSION

bibliography

As there are literally hundreds—if not thousands—of available titles dealing with UFOs, crop circles, cattle mutilations, and various other related phenomena, producing a comprehensive bibliography would not only be unfeasible but would make this a ponderous book in the process. As such, I am including only a small sampling of what's available out there, mostly based upon a particular book's timeliness and its author's credentials. By no means should this list be considered exhaustive, nor should the inclusion of these titles be construed as an endorsement of any of these works (or exclusion of particular titles or authors evidence of disagreement); I instead leave it for the reader to determine their value as a source of knowledge. Finally, copyright dates on most of the books are first-edition dates; some of the older books have since been reprinted—usually by other publishers—and so they often remain in print today.

Berlitz, Charles, and William L. Moore. *The Roswell Incident.* New York: MJF Books, 1997.

Clark, Jerome. *The UFO Book: Encyclopedia of the Extraterrestrial.* Detroit: Visible Ink Press, 1998.

Corso, Philip J., and William J. Birnes. *The Day After Roswell.* New York: Simon & Schuster, 1997.

Frazier, Kendrick, Barry Karr, and Joe Nickell, eds. *The UFO Invasion: The Roswell Incident, Alien Abductions, and Government Coverups.* Amherst, NY: Prometheus Books, 1997.

Friedman, Stanton T. *Top Secret/Majic: Operation Majestic-12 and the United States Government's UFO Cover-up.* New York: Marlowe & Co., 1996.

Hopkins, Budd. *Missing Time: A Documented Study of UFO Abductions.* New York: R. Marek Publishers, 1981.

Howe, Linda Moulton. *Alien Harvest: Further Evidence Linking Animal Mutilations and Human Abductions to Alien Life Forms.* Littleton, CO: Linda Moulton Howe Productions, 1993.

———. *Mysterious Lights and Crop Circles.* Jamison, PA: Linda Moulton Howe Productions, 2002.

Keyhoe, Donald E. *The Flying Saucers Are Real,* first edition. New York: Fawcett, 1950.

Korff, Kal K. *The Roswell UFO Crash: What They Don't Want You to Know.* New York: Dell, 2000.

Marrs, Jim. *Alien Agenda: Investigating the Extraterrestrial Presence Among Us.* New York: HarperCollins, 2000.

Pope, Nick. *The Uninvited: An Exposé of the Alien Abduction Phenomenon.* New York: Pocket Books, 1998.

Pringle, Lucy. *Crop Circles: The Greatest Mystery of Modern Times.* London: Thorsons, 2000.

Randle, Kevin. A History of UFO Crashes. New York: Avon, 1995.

Randle, Kevin, and Donald Schmitt. UFO Crash at Roswell. New York: Avon, 1991.

Randles, Jenny. The Truth Behind Men in Black: Government Agents—or Visitors from Beyond. New York: St. Martin's Press, 1997.

Ruppelt, Edward J. The Report on Unidentified Flying Objects, first edition. Garden City, NY: Doubleday, 1956.

Story, Ronald, ed. Encyclopedia of UFOs. New York: Doubleday, 1980.

Strieber, Whitley. Communion: A True Story. New York: Beech Tree Books, 1987.

Free Magazine

Read unique
articles by Llewellyn
authors, recommendations by experts,
and information on new releases. To receive a **free** copy
of Llewellyn's consumer magazine, *New Worlds of Mind &*
Spirit, simply call 1-877-NEW-WRLD or visit our website
at www.llewellyn.com and click on *New Worlds*.

LLEWELLYN ORDERING INFORMATION

Order Online:
Visit our website at www.llewellyn.com, select your books, and order them
on our secure server

Order by Phone:
- Call toll-free within the U.S. at 1-877-NEW-WRLD
  (1-877-639-9753). Call toll-free within Canada at
  1-866-NEW-WRLD (1-866-639-9753)
- We accept VISA, MasterCard, and American Express

Order by Mail:
Send the full price of your order (MN residents add 7% sales tax) in
U.S. funds, plus postage & handling to:

> Llewellyn Worldwide
> 2143 Wooddale Drive, Dept. 0-7387-1383-0
> Woodbury, MN 55125-2989, U.S.A.

Postage & Handling:

Standard (U.S., Mexico, & Canada). If your order is:
$24.99 and under, add $3.00
$25.00 and over, FREE STANDARD SHIPPING

AK, HI, PR: $15.00 for one book plus $1.00 for
each additional book

International Orders (airmail only):
$16.00 for one book plus $3.00 for each additional book

Orders are processed within 2 business days.
Please allow for normal shipping time. Postage and handling rates subject to change.

To order, call 1-877-NEW-WRLD
Prices subject to change without notice
Order at Llewellyn.com 24 hours a day, 7 days a week!

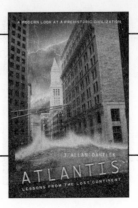

Atlantis: Lessons from the Lost Continent

A Modern Look at a Prehistoric Civilization

J. ALLAN DANELEK

Is the Atlantis story a myth, pseudo-science, or a true story with lessons for our future? Objective and scrupulous, J. Allan Danelek applies his signature no-nonsense approach to the legend of the Lost Continent.

Investigating Plato's dialogues, geosciences, traditional theories, and historical maps, Danelek attempts to answer the questions surrounding this twelve-thousand-year-old legend. Did Atlantis truly exist? If so, what was its culture like? How did the Atlanteans destroy themselves? Why haven't we found any evidence of this civilization? And finally, what can we learn from the fate of Atlantis—an advanced civilization perhaps not unlike our own?

This engaging exploration of Atlantis offers reasonable and fascinating theories of what may have happened to this ancient civilization.

978-0-7387-1162-1
264 pages   **$15.95**

The Case for Ghosts
An Objective Look at the Paranormal

J. ALLAN DANELEK

What are ghosts? Can anyone become one? How do they interact with time and space? Stripping away the sensationalism and fraud linked to this contentious topic, J. Allan Danelek presents a well-researched study of a phenomenon that has fascinated mankind for centuries.

Analyzing theories that support and debunk these supernatural events, Danelek objectively explores hauntings, the ghost psyche, spirit communication, and spirit guides. He also investigates spirit photography, EVP, ghost-hunting tools, ouija boards, and the darker side of the ghost equation—malevolent spirits and demon possession. Whether you're a ghost enthusiast or a skeptic, *The Case for Ghosts* promises amazing insights into the spirit realm.

978-0-7387-0865-2
240 pages
$12.95

UFO Mysteries
A Reporter Seeks the Truth

CURT SUTHERLY

Come face to face with the unknown.

Take a weird journey into the unexplained with fifteen gripping stories gathered from the author's own journalistic investigations. From alien encounters to eyewitness disappearances to the Mars probe failure, these are puzzles without real solutions.

Curt Sutherly points out significant parallels among sightings in different parts of the United States, which add up to a pattern of strange occurrences that cannot be intelligently dismissed—or forgotten. Learn the truth about these mysterious sightings and who's attempting to cover them up.

- A fast-paced tour through thirty years of the weirdest events to hit this country
- Written by an experienced journalist and ufologist who has interviewed and personally investigated many of the remarkable events he documents in this collection
- Contains fifteen gripping stories that run the gamut of the bizarre, from monster sightings to UFO cover-ups

978-0-7387-0106-6

264 pages $12.95

To order, call 1-877-NEW-WRLD
Prices subject to change without notice
Order at Llewellyn.com 24 hours a day, 7 days a week!

UFOs Over Topanga Canyon

Eyewitness Accounts of the California Sightings

PRESTON DENNETT

The rural California community of Topanga Canyon is home to eight thousand close-knit residents, Topanga State Park, and an unusual amount of strange activity going on in the sky.

Like Hudson Valley, New York, and Gulf Breeze, Florida, Topanga Canyon is considered a UFO hot spot, with sightings that began more than fifty years ago and continue to this day. This is the first book to present the activity in the witnesses' own words.

Read new cases of unexplained lights, metallic ships, beams of light, face-to-face alien encounters, UFO healings, strange animal sightings, animal mutilations, and evidence of a government cover-up. There are even six cases involving missing time abductions, and a possible onboard UFO experience.

978-1-56718-221-7
312 pages $12.95

The Psychic Adventures of Derek Acorah

Star of TV's Most Haunted

DEREK ACORAH

Now available for the first time to U.S. booksellers, this is the wildly successful story of Britain's most popular psychic and ghost hunter. Derek Acorah, star of the popular international television show *Most Haunted*, shares firsthand accounts of his encounters with some of Britain's most notorious spirits.

Find out how Derek met three of Jack the Ripper's victims—along with Derek's surprising theories on the identity of the "Butcher of Whitecha-pel." Get the inside scoop on a variety of the United Kingdom's most haunted places—Belgrave Hall, with its violently unhappy spirits; the torture museum in the vaults of Auld Reekie; and Tutbury Castle, where Mary, Queen of Scots was imprisoned. Derek shares fascinating psychic experiences, from meeting the poltergeist of Penny Lane to discovering the dark secret of the Pyramid Tomb to seeing a beautiful spirit woman shapeshift into an evil entity at Leap Castle in Ireland.

Derek also discusses mediumship, spirit possession, animal spirits, angels, and guides, including Derek's moving account of meeting his trusted spirit guide, Sam.

978-0-7387-1455-4
240 pages $14.95

Strange But True

From the Files of FATE Magazine

Corrine Kenner & Craig Miller

Have you had a mystical experience? You're not alone. For almost fifty years, *FATE* readers have been reporting their encounters with the strange and unknown. In this collection, you'll meet loved ones who return from beyond the grave, mysterious voices warning of danger, guardian angels, and miraculous healings by benevolent forces. Every report is a firsthand account, complete with full details and vivid descriptions.

978-1-56718-298-9
264 pages $11.95

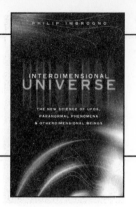

Journey of Souls

Case Studies of Life Between Lives

Michael Newton, PhD

This remarkable book uncovers—for the first time—the mystery of life in the spirit world after death on Earth. Dr. Michael Newton, a hypnotherapist in private practice, has developed his own hypnosis technique to reach his subjects' hidden memories of the hereafter. The narrative is woven as a progressive travel log around the accounts of twenty-nine people who were placed in a state of superconsciousness. While in deep hypnosis, these subjects describe what has happened to them between their former reincarnations on earth. They reveal graphic details about how it feels to die, who meets us right after death, what the spirit world is really like, where we go and what we do as souls, and why we choose to come back in certain bodies.

After reading *Journey of Souls*, you will acquire a better understanding of the immortality of the human soul. Plus, you will meet day-to-day personal challenges with a greater sense of purpose as you begin to understand the reasons behind events in your own life.

978-1-56718-485-3

288 pages $14.95

Astral Projection for Beginners
EDAIN McCOY

Enter a world in which time and space have no meaning or influence. This is the world of the astral plane—an ethereal, unseen realm often perceived as parallel to and interpenetrating our physical world. *Astral Projection for Beginners* shows you how to send your consciousness at will to these other places, then bring it back with full knowledge of what you have experienced.

Explore the misconceptions and half-truths that often impede the beginner, and create a mental atmosphere in which you become free to explore the universe both inside and outside your consciousness. This book offers six different methods for you to try: general transfer of consciousness, projecting through the chakras, meditating toward astral separation, guided meditation, using symbolic gateways, and stepping out of your dreams. Ultimately you will be able to condition your mind to allow yourself to project at will.

978-1-56718-625-3
264 pages $12.95